On the Road with Mary

On the Road with Mary

Stories of an Ordinary Family Serving an Extraordinary God

Beth A. Lenaway

Ordinary People Ministries

First Printing, 2023
ISBN: 979-8-9885356-0-7

Cover Image: Denny Driscoll
Cover Design: Katie Zeliger, Meraki Press

Printed in the U.S.A

Represented by Ordinary People Ministries
111 Greeves Street, Kane, PA 16735

www.OrdinaryPeopleMin.org

Dedication

First and foremost, this book is dedicated to our Lord Jesus Christ for without Him, none of this would have been possible.

Secondly, to the countless prayer warriors coast to coast who prayed often for this ordinary family as we sought to serve an extraordinary God.

Lastly, to all the dreamers. If God has given you a dream, step out in faith. You will be amazed at all God will accomplish through you.

Special Thanks

Special Thanks

Sandi Best	Creation of the Judean costumes
Ruth McClain	Stage Manager
Jim McClain	Base for the cross and pipes for the background
Missy Hartman	Paper mache rocks and Mary jug
Karlene Shimko	Original black curtains
John Shimko	Crown of thorns
John Bloomquist	Drink bowl
John Gentleman	Cross
Jim Nelson	Railroad spikes
Kim Rearick	Pony cart
Dennis Driscoll	Mary profile drawing
Al Denson	For encouraging me to "Be the One"
Pepperell Braiding	Pew ropes
Katie Yancosek	Prayers and editing
John Anast	Videography in NYC
Tom & Barb Hemdal	Being great aunt & uncle to the girls

Special Thanks

Original Accountability Team

Jim Peterson
Jim Nelson
Mil & Sue Reed
Barb Depto
Ruth McClain
Denny & Darlene Olson
Pastor John Shimko

Foreword
Jeff Nelson

I have fond memories of Beth calling me on the phone. I was referred to her by Al Denson as someone who could write music for her. With the amount of material that Beth had for me to write, my estimation would be that it would take me a couple of years to accomplish. I was thinking based on the average writing time of past songs.

When I mentioned the time frame to her, her reply was something like, "Oh no. God is going to give you these songs a lot quicker. We are going to get our little group to pray, and those songs will come quickly."

Well, to my surprise, all the songs came within a few weeks. It was like a download straight from His heart. It was obvious that His hands were on this ministry. What a blessing to have been a part of what Jesus was doing through Beth. All glory to God for all He has done!

Contents

Contents

My Beginning

"No Bethie... no... Listen to the note... listen! You are singing through your nose! Honey... can't you hear yourself? Let me plug your nose... it might help!"

So, what can I say? My singing career didn't start off with a bang! Oh, how my mom Bonnie used to work with me. My journey from "nasal to nice" was a nightmare!

Looking back on it now, I am so grateful Mom took the time to work with me. Who would have thought that all those hours spent hammering those notes into my head, in an attempt to get the same sounds to come out of my mouth would one day, many years later, be used by the Father in Heaven for His purpose? God did!

Jeremiah 29:11 (NIV) *For I know the plans I have for you declares the Lord, plans to prosper you and not to harm you; plans to give you hope and a future.*

{ 1 }

The Beginning

Luke 1:37 (CEV) *Nothing is impossible for God.*

From 1996 until 2006 my family and I were actively involved in a full-time ministry called "Ordinary People". During this time, with major help from my family, I performed a one-woman musical called "Mary – the Story of Jesus through the Eyes of His Mother". *Mary* was our "God Job".

Right from the very beginning, our journey into full-time ministry was filled with bumps, twists, turns, and even some flat tires along the way. It is our wish that by finally recording this journey of faith, you, as the reader, might gain hope and strength in your struggle to do God's will in your own life. If God can use us....an ordinary family from a little town in northwestern Pennsylvania, He can surely use you to accomplish His purposes.

So.... where does this journey begin? Let's go back to December 1985. My husband Jim and I were traveling to North Tonawanda, New York with our baby daughter, Kate (11 months old) to visit my Aunt Helen and Uncle Fritz Fehrman.

Jim and I were fondly reminiscing about "I Do! I Do!" a two-person musical we had performed several years earlier for Kane Players, our local community theatre group. What fun it had been working together to perform this two-person musical all about the ups and downs of married life. When, out of seemingly nowhere, an idea came to me! (We know all excellent ideas are actually Heaven sent!!)

"Jimbo... wouldn't it be cool if someone would write a musical about Jesus? Hey, Mary could tell the story of Jesus.... Mary was the only one who was there before Jesus was born and followed Him throughout his entire ministry. She was also present for his crucifixion and resurrection. Jimbo... Mary could tell the story of Jesus, her son. We could call the musical 'Mary-the Story of Jesus through the Eyes of His Mother'". This is how the idea of *Mary* first came to be and how God used an amazing series of events and people to get me to be willing to accomplish something incredible for His kingdom.

For the next few years, I did nothing with *Mary* except argue with God. I had a ton of excuses. Like – "Surely there were tons of people more qualified than me to write and perform a musical about Jesus." or "I teach kindergarten not music!! I don't know the first thing about writing a musical. I am no biblical scholar, God...I have a simple, childlike faith...' Jesus Loves me this I know'... or my personal favorite, 'God... I am too fat!'" Excuse after excuse after excuse... hoping that the still, small voice of the Holy Spirit would quit whispering, "Mary," and back off and leave me alone. Ha!!

In September of 1993, Jim came home from attending a "See You at the Pole" event at our local high school. The first words out of his mouth were, "Sit down Beth. God spoke to me today. We need to have a Christian concert for kids here in Kane, Pennsylvania in six weeks because that is the only Friday night the high school had available, and the concert has to be free."

When Jimbo told me his news, out of the clear blue (HA!) I said, "Call Al Denson – he will come!" Jim proceeded to argue that Al would be booked and that we had no way to get a hold of him and the chance of him coming to our little town of Kane was impossible and on and on and on. To which I replied, "Jim – just call Al Denson, he will come." "Beth...how can we call him when we do not even know how to reach him?" I suggested that Jim call Benson Records. Would you believe that Al's booking manager just HAPPENED to be at the record company that day, standing right by the phone!?! Would you also believe that the only day Al had available in his schedule was THAT FRIDAY NIGHT!?!

Jim and I brought Al to Kane through God's blessing and the generous donations of many kindhearted people from our little town. The kids of Kane and the surrounding areas had their first contemporary Christian concert. Al, through the grace of God, opened many eyes and changed many hearts that December night in 1993 by sharing the good news of our Lord Jesus Christ. Little did I know that God had a much bigger role for Al Denson to play in the life of this very ordinary person. Over the next couple of years, Jim and I became friends with Al, but it never really occurred to me that the Lord had a hand in the development of this friendship, and it was this friendship that would have a significant impact on *Mary*.

The Holy Spirit never gave up on me during this long process of preparing me to start *Mary* for the Lord's kingdom. Almost daily

I would hear the still, small voice whispering to me, "What about *Mary?*" Still, I felt so inadequate, so insignificant. How could I, Beth Lenaway, possibly write and perform a musical? Why...I am just an ordinary person.

About this same time, I had been reading through the book of Ephesians in my Bible. I came to some notes I had taken on a sermon Dr. Robert Schuller had delivered on January 19, 1992. The thrust of his text was- "I Can't! God Can! Let Him!" I felt like I had been hit on the head with a ton of bricks. It was true.... I could NOT write *Mary*, but God could if I let Him. From this moment on, I surrendered to the will of God and said, "OK...FINE...you want me to write a musical??? FINE!!!" I am a little embarrassed to say that I even fought with God over submitting to HIS will for my life....what a losing battle, huh?

Within weeks of submitting to the will of God with *Mary*, my mom Bonnie whom I loved and cherished as my best friend, was diagnosed with a cancerous brain tumor. My family was devastated, to say the least. I could not even begin to think of writing *Mary* now, not when my mom was fighting for her life. Mom's first brain surgery was as successful as it could be, given the fact that Mom's type of tumor was one of the worst you could have (a glioblastoma multiform-Stage 4). Also, Mom's tumor was located within the short-term memory portion of her brain which meant she would have to re-learn everything from how to fold clothes to turning on her computer at work. Yet she never gave up!! Mom was a fighter. She gained incredible strength from God and recovered at an unbelievable rate. She even learned how to drive again. The Lord gave us, as a family, another year with Mom. We had one more Easter, one more Thanksgiving, and even one more Christmas. I now realize that we, as a family, had to have that year so that we would be willing to let Mom go home to heaven, straight into the arms of Jesus.

Right after Christmas of 1994, Mom started to feel "funny" as she called it. She thought the tumor had regrown again and by the time she was able to see her neurosurgeon, several weeks later, the cancer had indeed come back, only this time with a vengeance. The night before Mom's second surgery, she sat me down at the kitchen table and asked me to promise her two things:

To lose weight, because I am, after all so much prettier when I am not so heavy. (How like a mom, huh?)

To write *Mary* because that is what I need to do for God.

Of course, I promised Mom these things because how could I not, when I did not even know at that point if Mom would survive her second surgery.

That night I went to the Lord on my knees. I begged God to help me. I said, "God, I know you heard me promise Mom that I would write *Mary* for you, but God, I never wrote a play before. I am not a songwriter. I don't even know a songwriter. Where can I find a songwriter in Kane? Please God – help me!" The answer came to me as plain as day, "ask Al Denson.... ask Al Denson." Well, I made the mistake of telling Jim. Jim told me, "The next time Al was anywhere near Kane, we were going to see him and tell him about *Mary*. If God said Al would help us with *Mary*, then help us he would!"

Mom's second surgery was not nearly as successful as the first. This time our family felt as if we were on a huge emotional roller coaster. We began living day-by-day, not knowing which day would be our last with Mom. We all knew that her time left on Earth was very short, yet it was so hard to admit because I just wanted to believe that God would make everything right.... that He would provide the miracle healing we so desperately wanted. Nightly, it seemed, I would listen to a recording of Al Denson's song "Peace Be Still" over and over and over...letting the words sink deep into my sad, hurting, broken heart.

After months of traveling back and forth nightly from Kane to St. Vincent's Hospital in Erie, Pennsylvania, it was decided to move Mom to our local Kane Community Hospital into a "swing bed", which was an alternative to placing her into a home for the elderly, as Mom was only 62 years old at the time.

In July 1995 we heard that Al was coming to Lewistown, Pennsylvania which would be close to Penn State University. Jim had me talk to Mom and tell her that we had the opportunity to go and see Al Denson and ask him if he would write the music for *Mary*. Interestingly enough, it was one of the few times that entire summer when Mom stabilized, and I have to believe it was because she knew we had to see Al.

When we saw Al it turned out that his room just happened to be in the same hotel as ours. Over pizza after Al's concert, Jim shared with him all about *Mary* and how the Lord needed us to do this musical for His kingdom. Jim explained that because I am not a songwriter, we needed his help. Al said that he couldn't write the score for a musical play. Then Al asked Jim if he was familiar with the song "Peace Be Still". "Are you kidding?" Jim said, "Beth listens to it every night. I'm getting sick of it." "Jim, I believe the man who wrote that song for me is the one who is to write the music for *Mary*. His name is Jeff Nelson. I'll introduce you to him." The songwriter for Mary is Jeff Nelson.

On August 27, 1995, several weeks after our time with Al, Mom went home to be with our Lord. Beginning on October 10, 1995, I began to get up at 3:00 a.m. daily before I left to teach kindergarten. With five different translations of the Bible in front of me, I would say, "OK Father, I am ready. What are You going to write in *Mary* today?" The script for *Mary* was written in two and half weeks by God and this ordinary person. Can you even believe it?

We met Jeff Nelson over Christmas vacation in 1995 in Franklin, Tennessee. I had the opportunity to tell Jeff about God's amazing grace with *Mary* and to actually read the script to him. Believe me when I say that God gave Jeff a window to my soul. I told Jeff that because *Mary* was from God I honestly believed the music would write itself once he started.

Jeff skeptically said, "Sure, why not?" Jeff, through the intervention of the Holy Spirit, wrote the music for *Mary*, sixteen original songs, in just three and half weeks! Jeff later told us that it should have taken him two years. Amazing grace, huh?

Months before we had anticipated ever being ready, we began to perform *Mary* for God's kingdom on July 19, 1996. Every single day for ten years the Lord amazed us with His unbelievable mercy and grace. He used the simple message of the Gospel, as presented through Mary's eyes to cross denominational walls in incredible ways.

In our ten years of being out on the road with *Mary* God opened the doors for us to perform in twenty-nine different denominations from Pentecostal to Presbyterian, from Baptist to Catholic for a total of over 500 performances.

We performed from Moosehead Lake, Maine to Tampa, Florida, from Exeter, Ontario, Canada to Portland, Oregon, from California to Georgia, and from Indiana to Mississippi until we had traveled through every state in the continental US except North Dakota.

As a family, we traveled thousands of miles in our red van pulling our pony cart. Then we traveled in Caesar, our 32 ft. motorhome. God opened doors for us to perform in a wide variety of venues. For instance, in nursing homes, behind prison bars in Cambridge

Springs, and even off-Broadway in NYC. Once in Atlanta the audience only consisted of the eleven members of the deacon board. We performed for 90 nuns and then traveled to perform for 45 Baptist pastors. Our largest audience was 1,500 students and teachers of the St. Marys, Pennsylvania Catholic school system.

The scariest performance was in rural Pennsylvania when we came face to face with evil. The funniest performance was at Transfiguration Church in Olean, New York where I invited myself to perform for the Pope at the Vatican.

I performed with lights... one million of them at a mega-church in Delaware, and without lights... in a small country church with electrical problems. In 110-degree temperatures with no air conditioning and in a 50-degree church in the middle of winter. Brrr.

I performed with the stomach flu where I would run off the stage between scenes to throw up and run back on. And another time with laryngitis where I couldn't sing a note and had to lip sync each of the 14 songs. I performed without a front tooth in Brockway and with a painful foot because I tripped over an extension cord.

I share these things not because I am anything special, which I am not, but because I serve an awesome amazing incredible God. When we are at our weakest that is when God does His best work if we will just let Him.

Luke 1:37 (CEV) *Nothing is impossible for God.*

Lord Lessons

1. If God is at the center of your dream, there is nothing you cannot accomplish together.
2. One of the hardest, most painful lessons I have had to learn in my life is that God sees my entire life's journey, from beginning to end, not just the small portion I happen to be walking through at that moment. God could have healed our Mom, Bonnie, and He did. Just not on Earth. This is not how I would have written Mom's story. I wanted her to be healed and healthy. She was the glue that held our family together. Mom is healed and healthy in heaven. She is just waiting for us to join her.

Isaiah 55:8 (CEV) *The Lord says: my thoughts and my ways are not like yours. Just as the heavens are higher than the Earth, my thoughts and my ways are higher than yours.*

Questions to Ponder

---

1. Has God given you a dream? What is that dream?
2. Have you accomplished your God dream? Tell us about your process from dream to reality.
3. Share one Lord Lesson you've learned from your life's journey.
4. If you haven't accomplished your God-given dream, what is holding you back?
5. What baby steps can you take today to turn your God dream into a reality?
6. Have you ever lost someone you love? Have you ever prayed to the Father for healing only to be told "No"? How did that make you feel? What did you do with those feelings?

{ 2 }

The Adventure Begins

First Baptist Church, Kane, PA

Philippians 4:13 (NIV) *I can do all this through him who gives me strength.*

The stage was set. A simple black curtain, a rock, a small wooden manger, and an old timber cross had replaced the pulpit and communion table. The spotlights were in place. Two blue, one white and one red were ready to offer just the right effects.

The sound was ready to go. Track in the CD player, speakers plugged in and the cords gaff-taped down by my Dad, Bob Yancosek. Jim was manning the controls, eagerly awaiting the cue to begin.

The costumes were freshly pressed and hung up in order. These were designed and created by my dear friend Sandi Best and were ready to be put on at a moment's notice with the help of Ruthie McClain, my stage manager, taskmaster, and friend.

The products - offering a small remembrance - were attractively set out on the table by our daughters, Kate and Chelsea, who were 11 and 9 respectively when we began our ministry.

The congregation was packed with family and friends, all eagerly anticipating the premiere of the musical drama they had been lifting up in their prayers for months. They were here to witness the fulfillment of a dream and the birth of a new ministry, Ordinary People.

The months of preparation, perspiration, prayer, and practice were now over. All that was left was for me, Beth Ann Lenaway, to walk down the aisle, water jug in hand, to begin my God job – *Mary*.

Oh Lord, I think I am going to be sick.

I am so unworthy to portray your Mom. God, are you sure you didn't choose the wrong gal? How can I portray *Mary*? I am a teacher, not a performer. I think I am going to be sick. I need Imodium. I can't do this. I'm too old. I'm too fat.

Wait. Oh no! Jimbo is playing my entrance music. Now I have to go. Oh dear. God help me.

What can I say except my first performance of *Mary, the Story of Jesus through His Mother's Eyes* came and went.

Now, in retrospect, opening night is pretty much a warm, fuzzy blur in my scrapbook of life with the exception of the two, crystal-clear "Lord Lessons".

Philippians 4:13 (CEV) *Christ gives me the strength to face anything.*

Lord Lessons

1. Even though in that first performance I forgot to sing the theme song of our entire ministry called "Ordinary People" no one noticed, not even Jim who was following along in the script. I would later learn that the Gospel, the Good News of our Lord Jesus Christ is so powerful, that all other things pale in comparison- things like forgotten words, broken spotlights, funky sound, costume malfunctions, and missed cues. It is the message that matters, not the outward circumstances.

2. God confirmed to me that this method of theater - where I communicate in the first person with the audience as one talks to a close friend and through the use of minimal staging – forces the audience to use their imaginations as *Mary* transports them back in time to the city of Nazareth. They begin to see the life of Jesus through His mother's eyes.

By portraying *Mary* in the first person, as the mom she was, the audience was able to sympathize with the real pain Mary felt as she birthed Jesus, her baby boy who was born to die for our sins.

Also, the audience was able to empathize with Mary because we all have a mom, or have been blessed with children ourselves.

Here are two examples: First, when asked how she liked the musical, Julia Montgomery, a dear Catholic friend who has since gone home to be with Jesus, said, "It was the first time I saw Mary as someone other than a porcelain statue."

Second, when asked if he could name the characters he had seen in the musical, my little friend Isaac Brocious who was about six at the time said, "I saw Mary, Joseph, Jesus, the wise men. And I saw John the Baptist, the disciples, and Judas." Amazing that Isaac could "see" all those characters considering that *Mary* is a one-woman musical.

Questions to Ponder

In the Contemporary English Version (CEV), Philippians 4:13 states, *"Christ gives me the strength to face anything."* I had so many fears to face on that opening night so long ago-fears of inadequacy, unworthiness, and failure.

1. What is it that God is calling you to face? (Be specific)
2. What detailed step-by-step plan can God and you design to overcome the giants you are facing?
3. The Bible is filled with ordinary people who were called upon by God to accomplish the extraordinary. Can you name some of these folks and what they accomplished with the Holy Spirit's help?
4. Why does God so often choose ordinary people to accomplish His tasks?

{ 3 }

The Great Adventure

United Methodist Church, Port Allegheny, Pennsylvania

John 15:1-2 (NIV) *I am the true vine, and my Father is the gardener. He cuts off every branch in me that bears no fruit, while every branch that does bear fruit he prunes so that it will be even more fruitful.*

1 Peter 1:6-7 (NIV) *In all this you greatly rejoice, though now for a little while you may have had to suffer grief in all kinds of trials. These have come so that the proven genuineness of your faith—of greater worth than gold, which perishes even though refined by fire—may result in praise, glory and honor when Jesus Christ is revealed.*

Thus began what I lovingly refer to as "the great adventure." From humble beginnings, we began to perform *Mary* almost every weekend learning invaluable insights or "Lord Lessons" every step of the way.

In that first year of ministry, God continually pruned (John 15:12) and refined (1 Peter 1:6,7) us, often putting us in situations where we would have to totally rely on Him.

One of our first performances after our memorable grand opening weekend in Kane saw us traveling to the United Methodist Church in Port Allegheny, Pennsylvania. Even though "Port", as it is nicknamed, was only 34 miles away from Kane, the Lenaway family was on our first road trip.

We pulled into the parking lot of the church with our red caravan and my Dad, Bob's truck loaded to the hilt. We arrived four hours early because we had never set up our equipment in any other church besides our home church. We had no clue how long our setup would take us.

Well, 3 hours and 55 minutes later we finished with a whole five minutes to spare! Thankfully, as time went on, set up got to be old hat.

The musical was set to begin at 7:00 p.m. Well, 7:00 came and went with only 15 people in attendance. It seemed *Mary* had been scheduled at the same time as the Fireman's Carnival in Port Alleghany. To go from performing for literally hundreds of folks the weekend before to 15 people was humbling. Then to make matters worse those 15 individuals were scattered all over the church. One here, two there, three in the last pew. No one sitting in the front pews of the church which shows that some things never change. How was I to interact with these folks, to have them become Mary's friends if I had to run all over the church just to make eye contact?

To be honest, this was not my best performance of *Mary*. I am ashamed to say I let the low attendance shake me to the core. I forgot the words, I forgot the songs, I had to ask to start over on one song three times.

Golly, what a humiliation.

John 15:1-2 (CEV) *Jesus said to his disciples: I am the true vine, and my Father is the gardener. He cuts away every branch of mine that doesn't produce fruit. But he trims clean every branch that does produce fruit, so that it will produce even more fruit.*

1 Peter 1:6-7 (CEV) *On that day you will be glad, even if you have to go through many hard trials for a while. Your faith will be like gold that has been tested in a fire. And these trials will prove that your faith is worth much more than gold that can be destroyed. They will show that you will be given praise and honor and glory when Jesus Christ returns.*

Lord Lessons:

1. When I perform, I am performing for an audience of one – our Lord Jesus Christ. It does not matter if there are 10 people in attendance at *Mary* or 1,000 people. I still perform for only one – my Lord.
2. Forgetting the theme song of *Mary*, stumbling over words, and on and on. This was not the only time God used what I learned to call "The Great Humbling" (TGH) to get my attention. You will see TGH as a consistent theme throughout these adventures.
3. We were given a set of maroon ropes by our friends at Pepperell Braiding in Bradford, Pennsylvania. We used those ropes for every single performance from then on out to rope

off the back half of the venue so that everyone had to sit down in front. Interesting that we had pastors from every denomination offer to buy our ropes. I wonder if there is rear seating in Heaven. Tee! Hee!

Questions to Ponder

1. I call the times when the Lord gets my attention "The Great Humbling" or TGH. Can you recall a time when you got a bit too full of yourself and God intervened? Tell us about your experience.
2. What did you learn? What was your takeaway?
3. Search your heart for what motivates you daily in your job, your ministry, your family, etc.
4. Do you strive for earthy acceptance and accolades? Why or why not?
5. Whose approval do you seek? Man's or God's? Explain your choice.

{ 4 }

New England in Autumn

Moosehead Lake, Maine

Matthew 28:19-20 (NIV) *"Therefore go and make disciples of all nations baptizing them in the name of the Father and of the Son of the Holy Spirit and teaching them to obey everything I have commanded you. And surely, I am with you always, to the very end of the age."*

Autumn in New England has been a lifelong dream of mine. Who would have ever guessed my family and I would have the opportunity to take our first big *Mary* road trip? We traveled throughout New England which included a *Mary* performance in Moosehead Lake, Maine.

God had truly been working in my life and the lives of my family. At this point in the ministry, God had provided us with a utility trailer through the generosity of Kim and John from

Kittanning, Pennsylvania. A trailer six feet tall, designed solely so my costumes could hang free from wrinkles.

To have strength and stability while being taller than it is wide, the trailer had to be shaped like a horse trailer. Consequently, it was nicknamed "pony cart." People often asked if there was a donkey inside.

Let me back up and tell you that I was granted a yearlong sabbatical from my school district to be able to travel the United States. Interestingly enough, it was the last such travel sabbatical my school district was able to grant. Right after my approval, the Pennsylvania Department of Education decided that educators could only take sabbaticals for health reasons and for furthering education. Yes, God's timing is always perfect!

Jimbo and I would fill these road trips with many varied and exciting educational experiences for our daughters because every time we went on a trip, we would need to take Kate and Chelsea out of school to travel with us.

This trip was no exception. On our way to Maine, we took several days out to explore Boston, Plymouth Rock, the Mayflower, and Plymouth Plantation. And we also embarked on a whale watch. To this point, we had only seen pictures of whales. I still get misty when I think back to the huge, amazing mammals breaching up into the air, putting on quite a show for the Lenaway foursome.

From Boston, we moved down the coast a bit to board a ferry that would take us to explore the wonders of Nantucket. You know I have often seen paintings of little cottages with roses blooming all over their roofs and, quite frankly, I figured the paintings were simply the product of an artist's vivid imagination- that is, until we went to Nantucket. There were those rose-covered cottages... simply gorgeous. It was a day I will never forget.

We also watched the carving of scrimshaws, and the making of lightship baskets. Then we found out how fast we could devour a lobster. Yum!

Once we were back on the mainland, we toured right up the coast into Acadia National Park which is near Bar Harbor, Maine. The park was beautiful, especially in the fall. One of the favorite sights in the park is called "Thunder Hole." Although the day we walked down to see it, it was too calm for the hole to do anything but trickle. We want to go back to "Thunder Hole" when the water is rough so that we can hear the thunder of the water as it rushes up to the rocky shore. Acadia National Park with its high rocky shores and pounding surf is exactly how I imagined the rocky coast of Maine.

Other highlights on our way to Moosehead Lake included finding the Gorton Fisherman in Gloucester and touring the grounds of Hammond Castle (of the Hammond organ fame) which is said to be haunted by several ghosts.

When we finally arrived in Moosehead Lake, it happened to be the final day of moose hunting season. Of course, what do we see pulling into the local minimart in the back of a flatbed truck? A gigantic moose. A gigantic dead moose!

We grabbed a bite to eat before heading off for our evening performance of *Mary*. Interestingly enough, the local McDonalds closes at 7:00 PM in the off-season.

We were warmly welcomed by the pastor, his family, and regulars of the Church of the Open Bible. It was such a unique experience to perform *Mary* in a place where much of the town's population is tourists. In October, Moosehead Lake was not exactly over-populated.

One of the most unusual things about performing in Maine was that they told us to be aware of the moose. A full-grown bull moose would stand taller than our Dodge Caravan and utility trailer. We were told not to be concerned if a moose walked along beside our car for they are very curious. Fortunately, we had no curious moose come to investigate us. Whew!

You may be intrigued as to how we were able to end up performing *Mary* in Maine and throughout the United States and Canada. Jimbo has vast experience in sales and marketing, so he created a warm referral system. After every performance, we would inform the audience that if they knew of a church that they felt would welcome *Mary* to complete a referral form. Soon we had hundreds of recommendations for churches in numerous states. It was as if God opened up the floodgates for our simple family ministry to spread the good news.

Matthew 28:19-20 (CEV) *Go to the people of all nations and make them my disciples. Baptize them in the name of the Father, the Son, and the Holy Spirit, and teach them to do everything I have told you. I will be with you always, even until the end of the world.*

Once again, I needed and received some more...

Lord Lessons

1. When God is in the center of your dreams, there is nothing that He can't accomplish through you.

2. The warm referral system Jimbo had us use after every performance helped open the doors for us to perform *Mary* hundreds and hundreds of times all over the United States and Canada. These performances were done when they fit into our family life and schedules without the need to hire a manager or agent.

Questions to Ponder

In Matthew 28:19 (NIV), *we are told to go to the people of the world and make disciples.*

1. How can you accomplish this?
2. Describe how God is calling you to a ministry like He did the Lenaway foursome.
3. How can you simply invite your neighbor to church?

Matthew 28:20 states, *"I will be with you always, even until the end of the age."*

1. How does knowing God is with you propel you toward action in your life's calling?

{ 5 }

Ninety Nuns and a Baptist

Erie, Pennsylvania

Matthew 5:5 (NIV) *Blessed are the meek for they will inherit the earth.*

On West Ridge Road in Erie, Pennsylvania there is a beautiful home for Catholic nuns called the Sisters of St. Joseph House. Imagine our delight when they called to see if Ordinary People Ministries would be available to come to the Sister House to perform *Mary*. The sisters wished to use *Mary* as a vehicle to invite and unify the surrounding community at large as well as a way to minister to their own sisterhood.

Now please understand, that the Sisters of St. Joseph have been working with the Erie Diocese since 1860. They have a remarkable history of ministering to the sick, the elderly, and the orphaned as well as providing education through teaching to the young and old alike. To say that I was greatly humbled and incredibly honored that they would want me, an ordinary Baptist girl to perform for all of them was amazing. Had they ever thought of Mary as a mom, a simple handmaiden, an ordinary person or would they find our portrayal of Mary as offensive or disrespectful?

Needless to say, I managed to work myself up into quite a tizzy by our performance date but then...

Philippians 4:6 (NIV) – Do not be anxious about anything, but in every situation, by prayer and petition, with thanksgiving, present your requests to God.

We were enveloped in love from the moment we walked through the front doors of the St. Joseph's Sister House. The facility truly is breathtaking but that is not what struck me. I cannot remember a time prior to this performance or any time since when I have felt such unconditional love. There was never a need to fear.

My family was whisked away to a private dining area where a multiple-course feast had been prepared for us and served on silver platters no less.

Kate and Chelsea were taken on a tour of St. Joseph's and given the freedom to do some investigating of their own (which they loved!).

Mary went off without a hitch after all of my needless worry. In fact, I can't remember a performance when I felt such unconditional support, empathy, and love from a gathering of folks. It was as if the Sisters of St. Joseph were able to place themselves in Mary's shoes, to feel her utter joy upon the birth of her son Jesus, her complete devastation upon his crucifixion, and her sheer amazement upon his resurrection. That night I felt as if the nuns and this Baptist girl came together as one for a single purpose – to share the good news of the Gospel with all those in attendance. It was a night never to be forgotten... ever.

Matthew 5:5 (CEV) *God blesses those people who are humble. The earth will belong to them!*

Lord Lessons

> "God doesn't call the equipped, son. God equips the called.
> And you have been called."
> Rick Yancey
> The 5th Wave, page 128, Penguin

1. This was the first of many times throughout our ministry that God would place me in a potentially uncomfortable situation so that I needed to rely solely on Him.
2. The Good News of the Gospel has the power to transcend all denominations, religions, and congregational differences.

Questions to Ponder

1. Think back to a time when God asked you to do something that you felt totally inadequate to accomplish.
2. What was the task?
3. Were you able to accomplish it? Why or why not?
4. How did you feel in that situation?
5. Why does God ask us to tackle tasks with which we have very little or no experience?

{ 6 }

A Hands-On Experience

Tampa, Florida

Job 8:21 (NIV) *He will yet fill your mouth with laughter and your lips with shouts of joy.*

Luke 17:6 (NIV) *The Lord answered, "If you had faith as small as a mustard seed, you could say to the mulberry tree, may your be uprooted and thrown into the sea and it would obey you.*

Our next big road trip happened right after Christmas of 1997. Why not head to Florida while our hometown of Kane is in the throes of winter? But how to get there? Did we really want to live out of our minivan again stopping to spend nights at inexpensive hotels along the way?

Of course, we dreamed of having a brand-new motorhome that could easily and comfortably transport us from church to church but that just seemed like too much of a miracle to ask Him to provide for us. Well, not only did God provide us with a motorhome but the owners let us rent-to-own. Can you even imagine?

We lovingly called this old (1985), thirty-one foot stubby-nosed motorhome "Caesar." For the next several years, Caesar was our home away from home.

Oh, the adventures we had out on the road getting from place to place. Our family has so many Caesar stories that I could share with you like no air conditioning while it was 110 degrees in San Antonio, Texas, where the only way to keep Jimbo the least bit cool as he was driving in the blazing sun was to ring out wet towels and place them on his legs as the sun beat in through the front windshield. Or perhaps I could tell you about taking Caesar way up into the Rocky Mountains to Estes Park, Colorado. The elevation is 8,000 feet. As we traveled up the mountain road, our air mattress in the rear of Caesar nearly exploded from too much air pressure.

But I think that for right now, I would just like to share with you about our trip down south.

We had been traveling and performing for several days. That's how we believed God wanted us to run this ministry. Other than $50 to $100 for travel expenses, we would take up a "love offering" at the completion of *Mary* and whatever God's people would provide would be what we used to get to the next church and another performance. Amazingly the love offering was often the exact amount we would need to get to the next church. In the ten years of ministry, we never went without our needs being met. In one way or another, God provided. Jehovah Jirah.

Well for those of you who have traveled south on I-95, you know that soon after crossing into Florida, there is a Welcome-to-Florida rest stop that serves cold fresh squeezed orange juice. So, of course, we pulled over in Caesar and stopped for a little pause. We could not stay long as we still needed to reach Tampa before 5:00 as that was when we were scheduled to set up for the 7:00 production.

After a quick break to stretch our legs, Jimbo, the girls, and I crawled back into Caesar, eager to head on down to Tampa. Jimbo turned the ignition and we all heard "click – click". There was no mighty "varoom". Only "click" and silence. To access the engine of Caesar, Jimbo opened up the floor space between the driver and passenger seats. He began tinkering with some wires, tightening any nut or bolt that looked like perhaps it had come loose on our trip.

This was serious. What were we going to do?

We had to get to Tampa, and we had no extra money. We lived from love offering to love offering with no excess. One look on Jimbo's face said it all. We were in trouble. Big trouble. Jimbo had no idea what was wrong with Caesar. If we missed our performance in Tampa, how would we have money to get home?

The girls - sensing our fear - began to cry. Ole Satan was having a heyday with the Lenaway foursome at this point. I was filled with self-doubt and guilt. Taking a sabbatical from teaching to do *Mary* for what? To break down in an old motorhome hours from our next performance. What were we going to do?

Then from somewhere (of course, it was from the Holy Spirit) Luke 17:6 came flooding into my brain. If you have the faith of a mustard seed, you could say to that mulberry tree "May you be uprooted and thrown into the sea" and it would obey you.

A mustard seed, I have at least that much faith. "Ok Jimbo, Kate, Chelsea, let's get out of Caesar. Now place your hands on the front hood. We have to ask God to start Caesar again so we can get to Tampa."

So, there we were. Gathered around and laid hands on the stubby-nosed hood of our motorhome and I said a simple prayer,

"God, Caesar is broken. We can't fix it. And even if we could get someone here, we don't have any money. Only You can help us. Please, God, fix Caesar so we can take the good news of your great love to the folks in Tampa. Amen"

Jimbo looked at me skeptically and said, "Now what?" I said "Start her up. Get those seatbelts on girls. We've got a show to do!"

Jimbo hopped in that rickety ole front seat, turned that key, and ... varoom!

Caesar's engine sprang to life. Wow! This was the first of many times we would pray in faith believing and God would hear and answer.

After arriving at the church, the assistant pastor and Jimbo re-checked the wiring and found a connection that had come loose when the screw fell out. They looked through their toolboxes but couldn't find what appeared to be a very unique screw.

The youth group was conducting a carwash at that time. Lo and behold one of the folks getting his car washed was a fastener salesman who just happened to have a complete sample case with hundreds of screws, nuts, and bolts in his trunk. After searching through his collection, he came up with it. Can you believe it? Jehovah Jirah – God, my provider.

There is, of course, a little more to this story as if breaking down, praying, engine starting, and meeting a nuts-and-bolts guy wasn't enough for one day.

The church had inadvertently booked a wedding rehearsal in the sanctuary at the same time that we were to be setting up for the 7:00 performance of *Mary*. For obvious reasons, we could not set up a backdrop curtain, cross, manger, lights, and sound. So, we did the next best thing. We assembled everything in the parking lot so that whenever the wedding rehearsal was finished, we could rush in and set everything in place, ready to perform.

5:30, 6:00, 6:20, 6:30. It got later and later. We were nervous. A steady stream of cars began to fill the parking lot for the performance. Honestly, I was beginning to think we would have to perform our first outdoor *Mary*.

Finally, at 6:50, we got the nod from the minister that the wedding rehearsal was over and to come on in. Ten minutes! We had TEN minutes to set up a show that typically takes over an hour to set up. What to do? We had each of the guests that had arrived for *Mary* carry in a piece of the production – amps, speakers, lights, cross, manger, backdrop, and fake rocks. In it all came and at 7:02 Jimbo started the overture.

Catch your breath, Beth! Catch your breath! I remember praying, "I am so exhausted. There is no way I am going to be able to do this tonight, Lord, no way. It has been a roller coaster of a day, Lord. First Caesar breaks down – You start it. Need a specialized screw – You send a nuts-and-bolts guy. The wedding rehearsal runs long, we assemble set in 90-degree weather and the audience carries in the equipment. I hadn't even had a chance to do my vocal warmups. No way will this go well. It'll be a major flop. HELP!"

Needless to say, I was in trouble as a performer. Yet, I have noticed that it was during those times of extremes,-extreme illness (flu) in Akron, Ohio, extreme humbling in NYC, extreme laryngitis in Corry, Pennsylvania, extreme fear in the women's correctional facility in Cambridge Springs, Pennsylvania, extreme prejudice in Long Island, New York, and extreme emotional overload tonight that God did His best work. It was during those performances when I have had to step aside and allow God to work, that *Mary* has never reached more people, reminding me again that God is so in control. When I am at my weakest, God is at His strongest.

The performance was sailing along without a hitch. Jimbo and I were in sync. All was going great. The sound and lights were working well. I was able to remember my lines. In fact, all was pretty uneventful until towards the end of the play at the cross scene where Mary's son Jesus is dying.

On a normal day this scene is heart-wrenching, let alone today when I am just so tired, so weary. Here is a crucial scene of the musical. The cross scene. Silence in the church. The scene calls for me to collapse at the base of the cross sobbing for my Son. Then from seemingly nowhere over the speakers, we hear "Breaker breaker one nine, this here's the Ruptured Duck. What's your twenty?"

Bahahahaha. Good heavens, we had done everything to get ready for *Mary* except a sound check! The truck driver who had stopped at the traffic light just outside the church was very close. He was on a harmonic frequency of my wireless headset so his transmission came blasting through our sound system.

The audience burst into peals of laughter which just made the next scene, Jesus' resurrection, that much more glorious.

Job 8:21 (CEV) *And so, he will make you happy and give you something to smile about.*

Luke 17:6 (CEV) *Jesus replied: "If you had faith no bigger than a tiny mustard seed, you could tell this mulberry tree to pull itself up, roots and all, and to plant itself in the ocean. And it would!"*

Lord Lessons

1. There is a distinct difference between our wants and our needs. What a valuable lesson to learn. God supplied all our needs throughout our ten years of ministry.
2. When I am at my weakest, God is at His strongest. Just step aside and let God work through you.
3. God has an amazing sense of humor. In my case, I would often witness it when I was getting too self-absorbed instead of God-absorbed. (The Great Humbling – TGH) This time it was a truck driver on his CB.

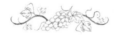

Questions to Ponder

1. Jehovah Jireh is one of the many names for God. It means "God, my provider." Remember a time in your life when God provided for you.
2. What happened? Tell about it.
3. How did it make you feel?
4. What did you do then?
5. Can you recall a time when God used humor to remind you that He is in control?
6. What happened? Tell about it.
7. How did it make you feel?

8. What did you do then?
9. When I am at my weakest, God is at His strongest. Recall a time when the Holy Spirit intervened because you didn't have the strength or courage to continue.
10. What happened? Tell about it.
11. How did it make you feel?
12. What did you do then?

{ 7 }

Mary Goes to Jail

Cambridge Springs, Pennsylvania

Matthew 25:35-36 (NIV) *For I was hungry and you gave me something to eat, I was thirsty and you gave me something to drink, I was a stranger and you invited me in, I needed clothes and you clothed me, I was sick and you looked after me, I was in prison and you came to visit me.'*

I have always been amazed at Mary. That someone so young would be so willing to accept the life path that God the Father set out for her with very little questioning. I read Mary's conversation with the messenger angel Gabriel in the first chapter of Luke with amazement. I paraphrase her response, "Whatever God needs me to do, I will do. Wherever God needs me to go, I will go."

Soon after we began Ordinary People Ministries, I wanted to try and adopt a "Mary heart"- a heart of willingness and obedience.

If a teenage girl is willing and honored to be the mother of the Messiah, then surely, I too could adopt a willing, obedient heart.

Whatever God needed us to do with *Mary* we would do it. Wherever God needed us to go to perform *Mary* we would go.

Within minutes of making that pledge (well, it was probably days, but it seemed like minutes) we received a phone call from the Cambridge Springs Women's Correctional Facility asking, "Would you be willing to go to jail to perform?" My thoughts raced. Ahhh.. no... me, in jail?... a state prison... I don't think so. But, what about the willing, obedient heart? Becoming more like Mary and less like Beth? I finally answered with a weak, "Ah, sure." The chaplain who issued the invitation assured me it would take at least six months to wade through the amount of paperwork it takes to get approval. Six months. I could be ready for anything in six months.

Ha.

Six months my foot! Six weeks to the day we were driving into the vehicular sally-port to be searched for contraband. We were scheduled to perform *Mary* for approximately forty female inmates.

We were given rather strict guidelines:

Our 90-minute musical had to fit in a 58-minute time period.

At precisely 7:00 p.m. the inmates would be locked down in the performance space with the four of us from Ordinary People Ministries (my Dad, Jimbo, Ruthie, and me).

We had until 7:58 p.m. to present the musical, at which time the inmates would be returned to their cells.

And above all else, do not touch the inmates! Under no circumstances. Do not touch the inmates. Oh no. *Mary* is all about interacting with the audience, including touching. How else could the observer become intimately aware of all that Mary went through with Jesus?

I should not have worried. From the moment I sang the first song about Joseph being a godly man, these women were broken. Many of the ladies found themselves behind bars because of some ungodly man. Then, when they met the baby Jesus for the first time, tears flowed. Because where were their babies while they were incarcerated? Not with them.

We finished with one minute to spare. It was an amazing night - one of my all-time most memorable *Mary* moments.

As the women were exiting the performance space heading back to their cells, Dad and I stood by the exit thanking them for coming to spend an evening with us. And, yes, we got hugs. Big bear hugs from the ladies as they left.

Oh, what a night!

Matthew 25:35-36 (CEV) *When I was hungry, you gave me something to eat, and when I was thirsty, you gave me something to drink. When I was a stranger, you welcomed me, and when I was naked, you gave me clothes to wear. When I was sick, you took care of me, and when I was in jail, you visited me."*

Lord Lessons

1. God will often push us to the point of uncomfortable. By doing this, we have no other choice but to rely totally on Him. I would never have been selected to perform at a women's state prison, but God had a plan to bless the women and teach me to trust Him more.

2. God's timetable is not the same as yours and mine. If He sees a need and you, through Him, can fulfill that need, He will make it happen. I was counting on it taking six months to take *Mary* to jail. I could prepare for anything in six months. Right? God gave me six weeks. Boom!

Questions to Ponder

Matthew 25:35-36 talks about helping our neighbors-feeding them, clothing them, giving them a drink, and caring for them when they are sick. I was given the opportunity to take *Mary* to jail.

1. What is it that God is asking you to do that might be uncomfortable in your own town or neighborhood?
2. List ways you can serve the people in your own community.
3. What prevents you from serving others?
4. God's timing is not the same as ours. If God sees a need and we can fulfill it. He will make it happen.
5. Can you tell about a time God used you to fulfill a need you felt totally inadequate to accomplish?
6. What did you do with those feelings of inadequacy?
7. Were you able to overcome them? How?
8. What was the result of "letting go and letting God?"

Amelia's Star

Olean, New York

Matthew 19:30 (NIV) *But many who are first will be last, and many who are last will be first.*

It began like any other performance of *Mary* with me fully costumed, visiting with my new "Galilean" friends, the members of the audience. Because *Mary* is written in the first person, I felt that it was important for me to establish a relationship with the audience before singing the first note.

As I was greeting everyone and welcoming them to "my village" I heard a commotion in the vestibule of the Bethany Lutheran Church. Of course, being curious, I walked back to investigate. It was there I was first introduced to my new friend Amelia. Her Mom told me that Amelia had come to *Mary* as a part of her birthday celebration. I was deeply touched and greatly honored that

Amelia would want to spend her 17th birthday with me. You see, Amelia has multiple challenges that she faces on a daily basis – nearly blind, having great difficulty speaking, as well as trouble walking to name a few.

Her Mom whispered to me that they would sit in the back of the church. This way, if Amelia needed to leave, they would not create a disturbance.

Now, how would Amelia be able to see if she had to sit in the back of the church?

I told them, "No," that Amelia should sit in the front pew so I could show her everything I was talking and singing about. Hesitantly, they agreed.

What a night we had that night. The louder I sang; the louder Amelia sang. Even though she had never heard the songs before, she gave a performance worthy of Carnegie Hall. It was so touching!

At the end of each *Mary* performance, we hosted a "cast party" inviting all in attendance to join us. It was a way to recognize that, by the end of the show, the audience members had become friends of Mary making them cast members in my eyes.

At the cast party, I gave Amelia one of our *Mary* show CDs which had all the songs and words on it as a small birthday gift. I told her the next time we returned to the Olean, New York area, she could learn all the words and help me to do *Mary*.

I never really thought too much more about Amelia until several months later I was back in Olean performing at the St. Marys Catholic Church. The audience and I were having our pre-show chat when I heard a commotion in the rear of the church. Upon investigating, I was thrilled to see Amelia and her family once again attending *Mary*. Only this time, they walked right up to the first pew, and this time, when I would sing, Amelia knew every word and sang right along with me. The louder I sang the louder Amelia sang. She knew the words perfectly.

At the cast party after the performance Amelia and her Mom came up to me. I noticed that Amelia was holding a little stuffed starfish! I couldn't help but think, "Ahh, isn't that nice... Amelia thinks I am a star. She got me a starfish; I am the star of the show."

Then Amelia's Mom said, "Amelia, tell Beth why you picked out a starfish for her. (Here it comes, Amelia is going to tell me that I, Beth Ann Lenaway, am a STAR! Listen for it.)

"Gah iz sta" (What did she say?)

"Gahd iz star" Ohhh God is star!

Not Beth. Not Jimbo. Not the girls or Dad.

God is the star of the show!

What a night, and what a Lord lesson to learn. God sent a multiply-challenged 17-year-old young lady to remind me that He is the star of the show. This musical is all about how great God is, not how great Beth is. It will be a Lord Lesson I will never, ever forget.

Matthew 19:30 (CEV) *But many who are now first will be last, and many who are last will be first.*

Lord Lessons

1. God is the star of the show – not Dad, not the girls, not Jimbo, and especially not me. Only God.
2. John 3:30 (NIV) states "He must become greater; I must become less." And in the CEV it reads, "Jesus must become more important, while I become less important." The more times I performed *Mary*, the easier it became to start believing the constant praises and accolades I received. To this day, sweet Amelia and her priceless gift of the starfish are vivid reminders of who the true star of *Mary* is... God.

Questions to Ponder

1. Tell about a time in your own life when the task you were assigned became more about you and less about God.
2. What happened to help you remember that any greatness we achieve is God working through us?

{ **9** }

A Vatican Invite

Olean, New York

Luke 1:38 (NIV) *"I am the Lord's servant,"* Mary answered. *"May your word to me be fulfilled."*

Another weekend on the road… but not too far from home this time. We were invited to perform *Mary* at another lovely church in Olean, New York. This time we were invited to Transfiguration Catholic church.

Our arrival and setup were pretty uneventful, thank goodness. We were greeted by a kind young priest who practically over-flowed in eager anticipation of the drama we were to present to his parishioners. His positive attitude was infectious. It helped all of us get into a Mary frame of mind. Tonight was bound to be special. We could feel it!

As soon as I was dressed in my first costume and make-up, I began my pre-show routine of greeting and welcoming each guest to Nazareth with "shalom." It has never ceased to amaze me that this simple method of greeting each person in attendance helps so much to establish a relationship between my new friends and me as Mary. This newly established relationship with the audience would come into play in a mighty way as Mary tells about her son, Jesus.

As I flitted around the gathering congregation, I noticed that I was not the only one in the church wearing full Judean fashion. Several visiting sisters from Africa (associated with St. Bonaventure University) had come wearing their full habits which ironically looked much more like my Mary costume than what we typically think of when we picture nuns wearing all black. The sisters and I could have been triplets which soon would prove to be very confusing.

As I chit-chatted my way towards the front of the church, I noticed our sponsoring priest sitting in a pew with several other folks. I decided to stop by for a pre-show chat. I greeted the older gentleman sitting on the end with "shalom." He wanted to know the name of the "order." "Order? Well, actually my name is Mary. I come from a very small village. Perhaps you have heard of it? I come from Nazareth."

The older gentleman looked at me suspiciously. The priest leaned over and whispered to me "Don't worry, he is from Africa. I will explain it to him later." Then he introduced some others sitting with him. One was a nun who was his mentor and friend. And the other sister was visiting us from Rome, Italy.

"Rome... Rome, Italy? Well, I am from Nazareth, but I would love to visit you in Rome. I've always wanted to go to Rome."

I guess you could say when I heard Rome, I kind of dropped character a bit, well alright, a lot! Mary probably would not have gotten so excited about Rome. Soon it was time for the production to begin. It was indeed a special night for all.

At the conclusion of *Mary*, the priest stood up and graciously thanked us for coming. He then began to introduce those in attendance with him: the guest priest from Africa, the Sister who was his great friend and mentor, and then the Sister from Rome. But what he had neglected to tell me earlier at the start of *Mary* was the Rome sister's place of employment. She worked for the Pope! I had just invited myself to the Vatican!

Hmm, they still haven't called.

Luke 1:38 (CEV) *"I am the Lord's servant"*, Mary answered. *"May it be to me as you have said."*

Lord Lessons

> "Wherever God needs me to go... I will go!
> Whatever He needs me to do...I will do!"
> *Mary*, Act 1, Scene 2

Adopting a "Mary heart" is not easy for me. I have a tendency to attempt life my way first; then, when it fails, go back and seek God's wisdom. I continue to be a work in progress.

Questions to Ponder

Mary was a young girl when she was chosen as Jesus' mom.

1. Why would God have chosen her?
2. What characteristic did Mary possess that made her favored among women as it says in Luke 1:28?
3. What does adopting a "Mary heart" mean to you?
4. How can you adopt a "Mary heart"?

{ 10 }

California, Here We Come

George, Washington & SoCal

1 Chronicles 4:10 (NIV) *Jabez cried out to the God of Israel, "Oh, that you would bless me and enlarge my territory! Let your hand be with me and keep me from harm so that I will be free from pain." And God granted his request.*

The Lenaway foursome was on the road again. Our minivan and pony cart were packed to the hilt, and the open road was before us. The good Lord was all around us- protecting and guiding our path. It was another *Mary* adventure.

This time our plan was to drive all the way to California, taking the northern route on our way out and a more southern route on our return. We planned stops at the Mall of America, Wall Drug (for free iced water), Mt. Rushmore, the Red Dirt Shirts of Idaho (the red dirt got all our clothes stained), "Dances With

Wolves" movie location, the Corn Palace, and the Gorge at George, Washington.

It also included several performances of *Mary* and attending Creation West (an outdoor Christian festival at the Gorge Amphitheater) which had been a longtime dream of Jimbo's and mine.

When I look back on our road trip out west, I am absolutely amazed at the beauty of America. God is such a master creator. Our nation is so diverse. For instance, in the state of Washington traveling east to west, you meander through flat lands with agriculture, through an arid region similar to a desert, and then on to a mountainous region. I had no idea, and I still would not have, had it not been for the opportunities God gave us through *Mary*. Traveling across America allowed us to observe the Master's fine handiwork.

I must comment on our visit to Mt. Rushmore. We arrived at the park just as the sun was setting after having spent hours in our van. Jimbo hustled us along through the visitor's center to find seats in an outdoor amphitheater facing the mountainside just as darkness closed all around us. "Ahh honey, are you sure we are not too late?" I asked. The girls whined, "Daddy, we can't see a thing." Then I said, "Look over there. I think that's Lincoln's nose or his chin." Jimbo being Jimbo just said one word, "Patience."

Jimbo no sooner got that one word out of his mouth when somewhere from deep within the bowels of this amphitheater a low rumbling baritone voice resounded. Captivating and mesmerizing all of us present. The stories of these amazing Americans immortalized in the mountain's stone began unfolding. Tears freely flowed down my face, as one by one, these former American presidents were illuminated until the entire mountainside was bathed in light. It was an "aha" moment for all of us. It culminated with the singing of the National Anthem as red, white, and blue fireworks danced across the evening sky.

A few days later, from George, Washington, we needed to head to Portland, Oregon where a couple of performances were scheduled. We decided to venture to Seattle on the way. While driving west across the state of Washington we encountered one of the sights that will remain with me forever. It was early morning, and the fog was just beginning to lift as we crossed the Columbia River and crested yet another hill. There, looming directly in front of us, was Mt. Rainier. Even though it was a hundred miles away, I felt as though I could reach out and touch its snow-capped grandeur. What an amazing and unexpected sight to behold. The spectacle gave Katharine Lee Bates' "American the Beautiful" new credibility because my eyes at last had actually seen "Purple Mountain Majesty." A vision never to be forgotten!

When I think back on this trip throughout America, I would be remiss if I did not share with you that not all of our performances of *Mary* were welcomed by those in attendance. In fact, in a little country church in central California, I first encountered folks so angry they actually got up and left before the performance began.

You see, in the publicity kit that we send out six weeks prior to a performance, the public service announcement and the press release explained to the reader that our good friend and Christian recording artist, Al Denson, portrayed the voice of the angel Gabriel – the pre-recorded voice of the angel. This family had come wearing their "We Love Al" tee-shirts and they left upset when they realized that Al was not there. It was only his voice. Thankfully, that was the one and only time that happened to us.

The highlights of this trip were so vast and amazing. Not only were the *Mary* performances such an honor and a blessing, but we will never forget things like sitting on the same stool at the same counter that Tom Hanks did in the movie "Sleepless in Seattle." We also watched fishmongers toss their fish through the air at the Seattle open-air market. We enjoyed our trip up the Space Needle. Crater Lake in Oregon was breathtaking. It was beautiful touring Napa Valley and seeing the colorful Victorian homes in Eureka, California. Driving through the Avenue of Giants, the redwoods towered over us in awe-inspiring splendor.

Another site to behold was the dozens of golden eagles that soared overhead in California's Golden Eagle Valley.

In Southern California, I enjoyed visiting Richard Simmons' exercise place. The girls loved the Jelly Belly factory tour and finding the Hollywood sign. We walked along Hollywood and Vine to see the stars of our favorite actors on the Walk of Fame.

Of course, we visited Disneyland and enjoyed a tour of the Crystal Cathedral.

You may wonder as the reader how on earth we were able to pay for all of these trips. Traveling with a family of four was indeed expensive. How was it possible to be able to get from our home in Kane, Pennsylvania to church "A" to church "B" and so on? Sometimes we were on the road for several weeks at a time. How was it possible given we performed for a love offering?

It was a huge leap of faith, actually. When we booked a church to perform *Mary*, we would ask the church for $50.00 to $100.00 to help with our travel expenses like gas for our little red Caravan and pony cart. (We didn't have our motorhome yet.) We would cash the travel check, put the money in an envelope, and use it when we were heading out to that church. Then, at the end of *Mary*, we would take up a love offering. That's how we paid for everything else from food to laundry to hotel rooms, if not provided. God is not called Jehovah Jirah – my Provider – for nothing.

Every one of our needs was met – every time. Ten years on the road and God provided for all of our needs and sometimes in abundance.

In Philippians 4:19 (NIV) it is written "And my God will supply every need of yours according to His riches and glory in Christ Jesus." My family and I are living proof that our God is an awesome God.

1 Chronicles 4:10 (CEV) One day he prayed to Israel's God, "Please bless me and give me a lot of land. Be with me so I will be safe from harm." And God did just what Jabez had asked.

Lord Lessons

1. Learning the difference between a need and a want can be a painful process but God will always supply our needs.
2. Not everyone will like you, and that's okay. God loves you! No. Matter. What.
3. America is God's gift to us. It is diverse, it is majestic, and it is awe-inspiring. Go. Enjoy. Be prepared to be amazed.

Questions to Ponder

Jehovah Jireh means God provides. This was absolutely true for us throughout our ten years in full-time ministry with *Mary*.

Make 2 columns on a sheet of paper. Title one "wants"; the other "needs." List your wants and your needs.

1. How has God provided for all of your needs?
2. God loves you but not everyone you encounter will love you. Sometimes not even like you. Can you share a time when you were not liked? How did it make you feel? What did you do with those feelings?
3. America is God's gift to us. Where have you been able to travel in the United States?
4. What has been your favorite adventure? Why?
5. Where else would you like to visit in America? Why?

{ 11 }

Photos

Beth and Missy Hartman, the theater director who taught Beth so much.

One of the things that caused "Mary" to have such an impact on people was Beth's personal interaction with audience members.

Poppy Bob - Beth's dad worked at most of the events by
helping set up and running the lights.

"Why did it have to be my son, God?"

This is the sign on the front of the Lamb's Theater.

More prayer team members: Sandy
Best, Shirley Fiero and Darlene Olson.
Sandy created all of the costumes.

Kate and Chelsea helped serve meals
at a Mid-town Manhattan soup
kitchen.

Many hugs and tears from dear friends like Robin Walters and others as
they board the buses to return home after the show.

Enjoying Creation West Festival.

The Great Humbling

The painting presented to us in Illinois.

Beth's final time as Mary performed at the Stable in 2006.

{ 12 }

The Lamb's, Lincoln Tunnel, Panty Hose & Carlos

New York, New York

Matthew 19:26 (NIV) *With man this is impossible, but with God all things are possible.*

James 4:6 (NIV) *But he gives us more grace. That is why Scripture says: "God opposes the proud but shows favor to the humble."*

Ever since I was a little girl and heard the incomparable Ethel Merman sing "There is No Business Like Show Business" I dreamed of performing on Broadway, too. Give me the bright lights of Broadway! Move over Barbara, Bette and Bernadette. There is a new "B" in town, and her name is Beth. Ha! Ha! Ha! What a crazy impossible dream, or was is it?

Nothing is impossible for God. Nothing. Not even Broadway. But how?

Being on the road as much as we were, you hear things. We heard of an off-Broadway theatre near Times Square on West 44th Street called The Lambs Theatre that had been known to welcome Christian actors to perform in their theatre. So, of course, off Jimbo, the girls and I went to meet with Jim and Dustee Hullinger, The Lambs Theatre managers.

The Hullingers were happy to let us come to The Lambs to perform *Mary* in the smaller of their two facilities. We laid out a budget for renting the little black box space and, including travel, meals, hotel, equipment rental, etc., would "only" cost $10,000.00 for a five-day run. So, if we charged $50.00 a person times 100 seats – voila! In just two nights, we would have the expenses paid for so the other three nights would be pure profit. We returned home with our heads full of possibilities and hope that *Mary* would have her "off-Broadway debut!" God, it seemed, would have other plans.

Jimbo and I attended the community Thanksgiving program in Kane soon after our return from New York City. Father Philip Pinczewski was the guest speaker that evening. I don't remember all of what he said except this, "You cannot put a price tag on the gospel. Give the bread away for free."

No! Surely not, God. We could actually make some money doing *Mary* in NYC and You want us to "give the bread away for free"? How in the world would that work, God? How will we ever get $10,000.00 to pay for the expenses involved in performing in New York for a week if we don't charge for admission?

Oh, me of little faith.

As soon as we put the word out that we were heading to New York City to present *Mary* for free to the hurting, helpless, and homeless, the funds started pouring in.

By the time our little family of four was ready to depart for New York, we had raised $10,004.00. Every cent needed was taken care of through the generosity of God's people.

Since we did not have to worry about selling tickets, Jimbo got in touch with many service organizations and social services in New York City. He invited them to attend along with the other theatergoers. They were able to bring van loads of their folks to The Lambs Theatre to enjoy *Mary* and be encouraged by its message of faith, hope, and love.

The day arrived for us to head for the Big Apple. It was August, and very hot. Our nerves were on edge a bit. As we were driving along Route 3 in New Jersey as it merges with I-495 nearing the entrance to the Lincoln Tunnel, red lights were flashing on the dashboard of our Caravan. (We hadn't gotten our motorhome, yet.) Jimbo looked at the gauges and the engine was overheating badly. He quickly swung our van and pony cart into the little triangle of paint where the roads met. Traffic was whizzing by on both sides. He looked under the hood and realized that he dare not open the radiator cap. Fortunately, we had a gallon of water in the back. After waiting a few minutes for the engine to cool down, he poured some water into the radiator.

His face showed that he was very concerned. I asked, "What do we do?" He answered, "We don't dare go into the tunnel with an engine that might overheat again. Let's find a garage." We exited into the Hoboken area desperate for a garage that was open. We found a Cadillac dealer. We pulled into the service area and spoke to their manager. After a while, he asked us to unhook the trailer and pull it in so his mechanic could have a look. He explained that it may be a while before they know anything. So, we went across the street to get something to eat and some air conditioning.

Back in the service area waiting room, we fretted for a few more hours. Could they fix it? How much would it cost? I turned to the family and said, "We need a huge answer to prayer. Join hands with me."

Eventually, the manager and two mechanics came out to the counter with paperwork. We went up as they told us that the fan module relay had gone bad. Jimbo was looking down at the page of the costs. It added up to several hundred dollars, but he couldn't see the final amount due because the manager had it covered. We knew something was up because the mechanics were grinning at each other. Finally, he unveiled the amount due. Zero.

What?

He told us that the fan module relay was on recall from Chrysler and there was no charge.

We cheered. We thanked them. We thanked God. We then headed through the Lincoln Tunnel to mid-town Manhattan.

After checking in to our hotel, the next day we set up the stage, and performed our sound check. It was finally curtain time for my New York City debut.

I wish I could say to you, my friends, that I humbly and graciously took to the stage on opening night at The Lambs Theatre. But to be honest, I was totally full of myself. I guess you could say "I thought I was all that and a bag of chips."

God was not having any part of that. It was time for The Great Humbling.

Up to this point, I had performed *Mary* hundreds of times in all sorts of circumstances without a single wardrobe malfunction. Not one time.

I would cover all my hair with cut-off pantyhose and then attach my headpieces to the pantyhose. My BFF, Sandi, made my headpieces with industrial Velcro so it would not come undone.

For an extra measure of precaution, I would also safety pin my headpieces directly to the pantyhose used to cover my head so there would be no chance of a problem. Until that night. My grand opening night, my off-Broadway debut. As I sat down on my rock singing the song "Ordinary People." I heard, "Rrrrrippp." "Oh no. What was that?" There it goes again, "Rrrrip."

There you have it, friends. I, Beth Lenaway, was performing with only pantyhose on my head. My industrial strength Velcro pinned to my headpiece had given way and, sure enough, I was left to perform the rest of that scene with "pantyhose head!" God has such a way of reminding me who deserves all the credit, all the time. Not "pantyhose head."

We were to perform *Mary* at The Lambs Theatre five times from Tuesday through Saturday evening. After the fiasco of opening night, I was hopeful that the other four performances would be uneventful in comparison. God once again had other plans.

The Wednesday evening performance had an audience filled with people who spoke very little English. Perhaps Henry Wadsworth Longfellow said it best when he said, "Music is the universal language of mankind." They may not have understood every word, but they knew enough of the scriptures to grasp that Jesus loved them enough to take their place on the cross.

Thursday night at The Lambs Theatre began as any other. Jimbo started the overture at 6:58 p.m. I prepared to go out on stage when into the lobby walked a young Hispanic man by the name of Carlos. "Hey, sister. I need someone to pray with me."

By this time, the overture had finished, and my entrance music had begun. Hmmm. What to do?

Looking around, I realized that I was the only one in the lobby and it was time for me to make my entrance in a one-woman show. What to do?

I grabbed Carlos' hands and we prayed while my husband played the entrance music over and over. He had no idea what was transpiring in the lobby.

I believe in so many ways this was a God test for me. Hundreds of times I portrayed Mary telling the gospel story of her son Jesus but in this instance, I had an opportunity to live out the gospel. To put feet on love. To pray with a desperate young man. Would his need for prayer trump my need to perform?

Carlos and I prayed. I learned he was jobless and down on his luck, not knowing how to feed his mother and himself. When we finished praying, I asked him to stay and watch *Mary*, which he did. Carlos returned on Friday with his mother to see *Mary* again. You will be happy to know that Carlos found a job helping out at The Lambs Theatre until he was able to get back on his feet. God is so good!

My favorite performance by far in New York City was the Saturday night show. Many of my friends and family rode eight hours on two charter buses to come and be part of *Mary* at The Lambs Theatre. Performing for my family and friends in New York City was an incredible experience. Jimbo had arranged to have a video crew from Bradford, Pennsylvania travel to New York to video this performance of *Mary*. When else would I get the opportunity to act in New York City again?

The two buses pulled in from Kane in the early afternoon and we took everyone on a little mini tour of the Big Apple. What fun! They saw numerous things from Wall Street to Battery Park to Central Park to Radio City. After a quick supper ala street vendor, it was time for the show to begin.

There was much discussion between Jimbo, me, and John Anast (the videographer) that night. Understandably, John and his crew were there to get the best performance they could. If I had learned no other lesson this week, I had learned God had me there for one purpose, to share the good news of the Gospel.

The video crew wanted to be able to retake scenes that were not my best. I, on the other hand, wanted to present *Mary* as the ordinary person she was. If there were flaws, so be it. For we were called to a much higher purpose with *Mary* – to present the gospel in a new way through first-person drama to folks who might not normally hear it, in places it may not normally be presented like in a tiny black box theatre on off-Broadway.

One of the people who had come on the bus was all the way from Pittsburgh actually. He was my dear friend Ruthie McClain's 77-year-old dad, Sam Douglass. Before *Mary* started that night, Sam led us in prayer. When Sam prayed, I believe heaven even came to a standstill. I have never met anyone to this day who can pray like Sam, an incredible man of God. Let's just say that *Mary* went off without a hitch that night. Was my portrayal of *Mary* perfect? No. But God saw me through every song sung, every word spoken. To God be the glory!

Matthew 19:26 (CEV) *There are some things people cannot do, but God can do anything.*

James 4:6 (CEV) *In fact, God treats us with even greater kindness, just as the Scriptures say, "God opposes everyone who is proud, but he blesses all who are humble with undeserved grace."*

Lord Lessons

1. God knows the desires of our hearts. Through Him, nothing is impossible, even off-Broadway. Luke 1:37
2. If you get too full of yourself, God will allow The Great Humbling. "Pantyhose head." James 4:6

Questions to Ponder

God is the God of the possible. We all have a God-job.

1.   What God-job has He asked you to complete for Him?
2.   Does it seem impossible? Explain.
3.   What steps can God and you take today that will help turn that dream from impossible to possible?

Mary Goes to School

St. Marys, Pennsylvania

Mark 10:14 (NIV) *Let the little children come to me, and do not hinder them, for the Kingdom of heaven belongs to such as these.*

One of the greatest joys I had as a performer was being asked to perform *Mary* for children. Anytime I was able to share my love of Jesus through Mary's eyes combined with my love of children and love of theatre, it was a win-win.

You probably suspect that I was asked to speak or perform at a lot of Catholic schools because of their reverence for Mary. And I was. I did everything from performing for 1,500 students, teachers, and staff in the Elk County Catholic High School gymnasium to performing for youth groups, the Confraternity of Christian Doctrine classes, and elementary classrooms. I was also asked to speak several times to public high school drama classes.

One of the aspects of our ministry that gave me such joy was when I was asked to do several of the scenes from *Mary* as well as share the story behind the production.

I absolutely loved to answer questions that the kids had for me. They certainly kept me on my toes. Then, I would get into costume right before their eyes, explaining that once I put my headscarf on, I would no longer be Beth. I would become Mary. What fun we had together- sharing about how great God is and that He only uses ordinary people to do His work. That way, God gets all the credit because, let's face it, if left up to us, there is no way we would be capable of traveling the countryside performing in hundreds of churches night after night. To be honest, I would be perfectly content just to hang out on the couch watching television.

That isn't how God works, though. God does not call the equipped, He equips the called. My family and I are living proof of that.

Mark 10:14 (CEV) *Let the children come to me! Don't try to stop them. People who are like these little children belong to the kingdom of God.*

Lord Lessons

1. God won't move a parked boat. Untie from the dock and sail, keeping your eyes on Jesus.
2. We can learn so much from kids if we will just be still and listen.

Questions to Ponder

In Matthew 19:14 (CEV) *But Jesus said, "Let the children come to me, and don't try to stop them! People who are like these children belong to God's kingdom."*

Or (NLT) *But Jesus said, "Let the children come to me. Don't stop them! For the Kingdom of Heaven belongs to those who are like these children."*

1. What does this passage of scripture mean to you?
2. Why do you think Jesus enjoyed visiting with children?
3. What can we learn from children?
4. Jesus states, "For the Kingdom of Heaven belongs to those who are like these children." What characteristics does a child possess that we could adopt?

{ 14 }

On the Road Again.

Christmas, Decatur, IL

2 Corinthians 2:9 (NIV) *Another reason I wrote you was to see if you would stand the test and be obedient in everything.*

It was time for the Lenaway Four to head out on the road again. This time we were headed to Decatur, Illinois to the First Baptist Church. You may wonder how we would get from Kane, Pennsylvania all the way to Decatur, Illinois. Well, as God would have it, the pastor of this church had seen us perform *Mary* in his former church in Bradford, Pennsylvania. When he was assigned to Decatur, he wanted to bring *Mary* to his new church too.

Of course, we were thrilled to go. I had never performed at a church in Illinois before. Why not?

As I was helping to pack up our caravan, I felt the Holy Spirit prompt me to take along our Christmas money - the money I had pigeon-holed away to make sure our family, especially the kids, would have a nice Christmas.

Wait! What? Not my Christmas money. $750.00

Geez. Ok, God. With half-hearted obedience, I put the envelope of money in our van's glove compartment and promptly forgot about it.

The Decatur church welcomed us with open arms for our Friday night performance. Thankfully, *Mary* went off without a hitch. The pastor presented us with a beautiful painting of Mary on canvas that hangs in our home yet today.

Bright and early on Saturday morning, we began our long journey home, when - bam - our Caravan started making noise and jerking! Jimbo could not get it out of first gear. As God would have it, we broke down near a Dodge dealer. I kid you not, Jimbo eased the van into the dealership's service area. Now what? My mind was reeling. Where would we get the additional money to fix the van? I was thinking that we needed a new transmission.

It was Saturday and the service department was open, but would they be able to fit us in?

God had blessed us with a love offering on Friday night but certainly not enough money to cover the cost of new transmission. What were we going to do? I was starting to get shook, when I heard the still small voice say, "The Christmas money, Beth. You have your Christmas money." God, what will I do for the kids' Christmas? "Just trust."

The garage fit us in on that Saturday. It turned out that we didn't need a new transmission. They only needed to replace the torque converter. When the bill came, it was $749.34.

God is so faithful.

Oh, and in case you were wondering about Christmas that year, we told our "transmission tale" after a performance of *Mary* in North East, Pennsylvania later that fall. After a few days, we received a check for $1,000 from a business in the Erie, Pennsylvania area with a note, "Buy your kids' Christmas."

Praise God from whom all blessings flow!

2 Corinthians 2:9 (CEV) *I also wrote because I wanted to test you and find out if you would follow my instructions.*

Lord Lessons

1. Trust... even when it doesn't make sense to you.
2. God knows and sees the desires of our hearts. He is looking for the faithful.

Questions to Ponder

2 Corinthians 2:9 reminds us that God will, at times, test us to see if we will follow His instructions.

1. Can you remember a time when God asked you to do something that didn't make sense? Please explain.
2. Looking back on that incident now, can you see God's mighty hand at work? Tell about it.

Performing for Man or King?

Estes Park, Colorado

Galatians 1:10 (NIV) *Am I now trying to win the approval of human beings, or of God? Or am I trying to please people? If I were still trying to please people, I would not be a servant of Christ.*

Psalms 115:1 (NIV) *Not to us, Lord, not to us but to your name be the glory, because of your love and faithfulness*

(Note: I am not proud of my behavior in this chapter, but it happened and has helped to mold me into who I am today.)

After several years of performing *Mary* from here to there and everywhere in between, I am ashamed to admit it did not take too long for me to develop a "fat head." My performances became more about me receiving wonderous accolades and thunderous applause, and less about telling God's story of Jesus through His mother's eyes, thus, encouraging folks to come to know Jesus and to get serious about their God jobs. Yep, I was overdue for another Great Humbling. I just didn't picture it happening in Estes Park, Colorado.

Jimbo and I received a flyer regarding an annual Christian Fine Arts Conference held in Ester Park. This conference and competition brought in the best of the best in all areas of Christian Fine Arts. The best singers, songwriters, producers, comedians, and dramatists were represented here. It was a chance to showcase your God-given talents. I, quite frankly, just knew that *Mary* would take all honors!

The conference was fairly expensive for two folks whose incomes relied on what was given in a love offering plus Jimbo's insurance commissions (he kept working while we were touring). But I felt that I should go to Estes Park and perform so that I could get the recognition "I" deserved. After all, "I" was out and about doing my God job every weekend. "I" was reducing people to tears with *Mary*. "I" was changing lives for God.

So, I convinced Jimbo that we just had to go.

By this time, our Ordinary People Ministries had purchased Caesar to pull our pony cart full of costumes and equipment.

Up, up, up, we drove high into the Rocky Mountains. It was amazingly beautiful. We learned several things as we drove upward.

High altitude does a real number on a twelve-year-old's molars. Poor Kate.

High altitude will cause an air mattress to expand greatly-possibly exploding if you are not careful.

Elk run around Estes Park neighborhoods like dogs and cats do back home.

It is important to use the right octane fuel, especially in an old motorhome, if you have hopes of getting where you need to go.

Finally, just like the "little engine that could," we chug, chug, chugged into Estes Park YMCA of the Rockies. I was ready to show off *Mary.*

We checked into the conference, and I wasn't there for five minutes when I began to get a little sick inside. No, it wasn't the altitude. The still small voice of the Holy Spirit was working on me. "Beth, why are you here? Beth, do you perform for man or Me? Why do you seek approval of others when it is my approval that should be all you seek?"

Oh, great, now what to do? We were there in Estes Park for a week. All paid for, and I made one of the biggest mistakes of my life. A costly mistake. I had forgotten whom I performed for. I didn't remember that I performed for an audience of one – the King of Kings. It is His approval I should be seeking, not the opinion of a drama judging committee. Oh, by the way, I did not win. I came in third at the competition. How humbling.

Galatians 1:10 (CEV) *I am not trying to please people. I want to please God. Do you think I am trying to please people? If I were doing that, I would not be a servant of Christ.*

Psalms 115:1 (CEV) *We don't deserve praise! The Lord alone deserves all of the praise, because of his love and faithfulness.*

Lord Lessons

1. It is very easy to get caught up in the mindset of how great I am and then forget that it is God alone who deserves all the praise. (Psalms 115:1)
2. My value as a person, as a wife, as a mother, as a performer is not dependent on the opinions of others. It is God alone that I will stand before when He calls me home.

Questions to Ponder

1. God first, family second and God-jobs third is a good priority list for life. How do your life's priorities stack up in comparison?
2. Is God first place in your life? Explain.
3. Do you put your family above your job? Explain.
4. Coming in third place is our God-job. Where is your job on your list of priorities? Do you need to re-prioritize your list? What steps can you take to make that happen?

{ 16 }

Po'Boys, Wi-ine, and a Little Storm.

Hammond, Louisiana

Matthew 7:25 (NIV) *The rain came down, the streams rose, and the winds blew and beat against that house; yet it did not fall, because it had its foundation on the rock.*

Winter in Kane is blustery, snowy, and cold. So, why not head where it is warm and the sun shines every day or does it?

January saw us Lenaways heading to Hammond, Louisiana to perform at the Victory Baptist Church. We got our first taste of southern hospitality. We arrived at the church in the afternoon and feasted on shrimp po-boys. Seafood at its finest. And the people! Oh, so kind and wonderful.

We learned a couple of things at Victory Baptist: At the feast at Cana, we learned that the word "wine" has two syllables in Louisiana. Jesus turned water into wi-ine! And we learned that 12-year-olds can drive as well as we can. Our motorhome and utility cart were parked near the side door. As we went to load in our sound equipment, props, lights, and costumes, it was dark so we couldn't see into the trailer.

I then heard one of the men say, "Junior, go get the truck and park here with lights on so we can see in the trailer." Junior immediately obeyed responding, "Yes, sir."

After that, we decided to head down to the French Quarter in New Orleans. We really wanted to experience this old city but probably not in a motorhome pulling our trailer down very narrow Bourbon Street.

From Louisiana, we made the trek to Hooks, Texas to stop in and visit Jim's brother, Eddie, and his wife Miss Ruby. We had such a wonderful time visiting them and their beautiful family. We even had the opportunity to perform *Mary* for them at the Everett Baptist Church. I remember this performance well because the church didn't have air conditioning. And it is hot in Texas, even in February.

From Hooks, we headed south to the Florida panhandle and Destin Beach. We were going to spend the night in a campground where you can park right along the Gulf of Mexico. On our journey southward along US Rt 331 we noticed a steady, almost bumper-to-bumper line of traffic headed north, away from the beach. We didn't think too much about it until we observed that there was virtually no southbound traffic toward the Gulf. Hmmm?

Finally, we arrived at a gas station at the corner along US Rt 98 to fuel Caesar. When Jimbo went to pay for our gas, the clerk asked us where we were headed. Jim told her the name of the RV park. The clerk said, "Aren't you worried about the hurricane?" "What hurricane?" Jim replied. She said, "The hurricane that will be coming ashore here tomorrow evening."

No wonder so many cars were headed north. And guess who joined them? Yep, we spent the night in Georgia.

Matthew 7:25 (CEV) *Rain poured down, rivers flooded, and winds beat against that house. But it was built on solid rock, and so it did not fall.*

Lord Lessons

1. If you travel, invest in a weather radio. We purchased one from Radio Shack the next day! (Now you can just make sure you have a weather app!)
2. There truly is something to be said for Southern hospitality and charm.

Questions to Ponder

The United States is filled with diversity from people to cultures to landmarks. Each region is unique and special.

1. If you could live anywhere in the United States, other than your current location, where would you live? Why?
2. What brought you to your current location?

Face-to-Face with Hatred

Somewhere in Pennsylvania

Ephesians 6:12-13 (NIV) *For our struggle is not against flesh and blood, but against the rulers, against the authorities, against the powers of this dark world and against the spiritual forces of evil in the heavenly realms. Therefore, put on the full armor of God, so that when the day of evil comes, you may be able to stand your ground, and after you have done everything, to stand.*

.

This chapter of *On the Road with Mary* is the hardest for me to write. Of all the experiences and Lord Lessons God has taken me through with *Mary*, one shook me to the core of my existence. In fact, for a long time, I stopped writing this book because of this chapter. Believe me, I wrestle even today as I write it, to even include it at all.

But, in an effort to be totally transparent, I need to share it.

By this point in our ministry, we had been performing *Mary* almost every weekend. God had opened unimaginable doors for us. It seemed every time I would say, "We will never perform for that denomination," God would open new doors. Everything was pretty smooth sailing with our God jobs. We had a routine and God continued to have us bless others through His production of *Mary*.

We were invited to perform *Mary* for an interdenominational group of folks on a Sunday afternoon.

Mary began as always with me out amongst God's folks welcoming them with "shalom" and a handshake or a hug. I remember reaching out to one person in particular and was greeted with a sharp "Don't touch me!" in a strange, almost sinister, voice. It was the first time in literally hundreds of performances that I had heard anything like it. Weird but I just passed it off as though perhaps someone was having a bad day.

The musical proceeded, and Mary was looking for Jesus when he was in the temple. It was a great time to draw in the entire audience as Mary's friends, looking for her son. In character as Mary, I was asking everyone, "Have you seen my son?" Yet, when I asked this same person, I felt as though I was staring into a black, bottomless abyss. I had never experienced anything like it before or since. Honestly, I was frightened and shaken to the core of my being. What was wrong with this person? God help me!

From deep within me a verse surfaced. "He that is within you is greater than he that is within the world." 1 John 4:4 I may not have understood what was happening at the time, but God did. And He was there!

Right in the middle of the play, I stopped the show and grabbed Jimbo, my Dad, and Ruthie. We prayed for God to release His angels, to protect us. And He did. I felt like I was given a supernatural power that day. I felt empowered by God to love even in the face of such apparent hatred.

I am not sure whatever happened to this person, but I pray to this day that somehow the love of God overcame her hate.

Ephesians 6:12-13 (CEV) *We are not fighting against humans. We are fighting against forces and authorities and against rulers in the spiritual world. So, put on the armor that God gives. Then when that evil day comes, you will be able to defend yourself. And when the battle is over, you will still be standing firm.*

Lord Lessons

1. There is hatred in this world. God is so much greater.
2. We are all called to love the Lord our God and love our neighbor as ourselves even if that neighbor shows us only hatred.

Questions to Ponder

1. We are not going to be liked by everyone we meet. In fact, there are those we will irritate or rub the wrong way. Share a time this has happened to you. How did you feel?

2. In Matthew 10:14, Jesus tells his disciples that if someone doesn't welcome you or listen to your message to "shake the dust off your feet and move on." We are only responsible for our obedience to God, not for the results of that obedience. We are the seed planters, but it is up to God and the Holy Spirit to tend to the rest. Share a time this has happened to you.

{ 18 }

Off the Road

Kane, Pennsylvania

Matthew 17:20 (NIV) *He replied, "Because you have so little faith. Truly I tell you, if you have faith as small as a mustard seed, you can say to this mountain, 'Move from here to there,' and it will move. Nothing will be impossible for you."*

Ephesians 3:20 (NIV) *Now to him who is able to do immeasurably more than all we ask or imagine, according to his power that is at work within us.*

Jimbo and I had always promised God, each other, and our accountability team that if and when we reached the point in our ministry where our daughters no longer could be out on the road with us, then we would make a change. Not sure what the change would be, but a change.

This happened after eight years in ministry. Our daughters, Kate and Chelsea, no longer wished to travel with us most weekends. I sure didn't blame them. They were in college and high school respectively and desired their own social lives. In fact, the last year we performed out on the road, I spent more time on my cell phone concerned about the girls' whereabouts than actually sharing the good news. This was a big problem for the mama bear instinct in me.

Even though they were good girls, everyone knew we were gone on the weekends, and this could have been a recipe for disaster.

A change was necessary. But what?

We arrived at a rather crazy idea- managing a theater in Kane. How in the world could we make a switch from bringing *Mary* to the people to bringing the people to *Mary*? Build a theater? How? Where? It appeared impossible.

Jimbo and I had no extra money. The love offering we took up after each performance of *Mary* always covered our needs but certainly never a want of such magnitude.

You would think after eight years of traveling ministry serving a God that had continuously blessed us, that my "doubt meter" would no longer be activated. But, alas, no. In fact, this dream of bringing folks to Kane to see *Mary* in some sort of theater so we could be home every night with our daughters seemed insurmountable, massive. This dream was unattainable for two ordinary people but not for an incredible God.

Matthew 17:20 (CEV) *If you had faith no larger than a mustard seed, you could tell this mountain to move from here to there. And it would. Everything would be possible for you.*

Ephesians 3:20 (CEV) *I pray that Christ Jesus and the church will forever bring praise to God. His power at work in us can do far more than we dare ask or imagine.*

Lord Lessons

1. If God is in the center of your dream, there is nothing He can't accomplish.
2. You cannot outdream God.

Questions to Ponder

1.   Paul writes in Ephesians that God is able to accomplish even more than we could ever ask for or imagine. In our case, provide a theatre.
2.   What God-sized dream do you have in your heart?
3.   How can God and you make it a reality?
4.   Is it time to untie the boat from the dock and sail out into your tomorrow?

19

The Stable is Born

Kane, Pennsylvania

Luke 2:7 (NIV) *And she gave birth to her firstborn, a son. She wrapped him in cloths and placed him in a manger because there was no guest room available for them.*

Jeremiah 29:11 (NIV) *"For I know the plans I have for you," declares the Lord, "plans to prosper you and not to harm you, plans to give you hope and a future."*

On the outskirts of our town of Kane, along US Route 6, sat empty a cluster of builders that once was home to the Ideal Farm. For years, folks would receive their milk from this dairy farm. More recently, Ideal Farm was transformed into the Holgate Toy Factory which manufactured the one-time world-famous wooden Holgate toys including Mr. Rogers' Trolley.

For the last several years, the farm and some of the buildings sat empty, devoid of any human life. It had become a wonderful playland for the barn swallows and pigeons that took up residence there.

Then one day in 2004, Jimbo and I learned that the property was for rent. Hmmm... Would it be possible to turn an old dairy farm/toy factory into a combination theatre/church/craft store?

It took an amazing God who knew the desires of our hearts, an immense amount of elbow grease, a ton of ingenuity, and the faith of a mustard seed. "The Stable" was born.

We felt the name was apropos, as that's where Jesus began also. The Church at the Stable, the Store at the Stable, and the Playhouse at the Stable became a reality. The Stable was home base to our production of *Mary* and so much more. It was the site of open-air Christian concerts, three show choirs, productions for Kane Players (our local community theatre group), summer dance camps, as well as home to a resident theatre troupe – the Stable Players.

The Stable hosted Sunday community church services. It also gave local crafters and artisans a place to showcase their wares in the Stable craft store. Tour buses throughout New York and Pennsylvania were making their way into Kane to attend our production of *Mary*. Life was good. So much fun and so remarkably busy. Until it wasn't.

In 2006, our landlord wanted Ideal Farm back. He had someone willing to purchase the entire site and turn it into a store. We had only weeks to vacate the premises. I am crying even now years later as I write this. How could God allow this to happen? Why did He so dramatically close this chapter of our life's journey?

After more than 500 performances of *Mary*, it was time to pack away the costumes and props. The dream of having a performing arts and worship center had turned into a nightmare. We needed to close the doors of the Stable and with that, I closed the doors on my creative self and pretty much threw away the key.

Looking back on it now, I can't really think about this time in our life's journey without getting emotional. The end of a long and important season of ministry was coming to a close. One that encompassed ten years of my life. And now what?

I had only known performing, singing, and directing for years. Now where do I turn?

Thus, began years of wandering in the great wilderness of life. I sure hope it will not take forty years like it took Moses and the Israelites. During this time, I felt barren of joy. I quit singing and acting. What was my purpose? Did I even have one anymore?

I felt like I was losing my grip on everything that had been so familiar for so long. Where do I go from here? I was certainly at a crossroads.

The first thing Jimbo and I needed to do was find a new church home. We visited several churches after the Stable closed trying to find the right fit. Finally, we discovered Open Arms, a Free Methodist Church in Bradford, Pennsylvania to call home. I didn't realize how exhausting being in full-time ministry could be. I was very weary. Attending Open Arms was quite nice because we could show up, join in singing a few praise songs, learn from God's word and just be in God's presence.

The church family there provided a safe, healing, and restorative space.

The next item on my agenda was finding a job. I went back to the one thing that felt somewhat normal – teaching. I began dipping my toe in the water by substitute teaching for a year in my former school district of Kane. Eventually, I went to teach at the Kane Community Pre-School in the mornings and taught incarcerated men and women at the McKean County Jail in the afternoons. Once a week at the jail, Jimbo would host a Christian 12-step program for the men.

Two years later, my friend and Superintendent of schools for the St. Marys School District, Annie Kearney, hired me to be the in-school suspension teacher. After that job, I started driving to Dubois, Pennsylvania for almost two years to help autistic children at Stepping Stones. The prospect of driving through another winter to Dubois (100 miles roundtrip) was not appealing to me at all. As much as I loved working with my autistic kiddos, when the position of Senior Center Director in Kane became available, a block from our house, I jumped at the chance.

I have been working at the Kane Senior Center for the Office of Aging since 2012 and my old folks have taught me more than I could ever teach them. Every day is a learning experience for my seniors and me. Unless something earth-shattering happens, I plan on staying at the center until I retire.

As I write this, Jimbo is 70 years old and finally retiring from Kane Innovations as their Sales Manager. But God threw us a new curve. Jim was appointed pastor of the small Bradford Free Methodist church called B-Free where I team up with him as the music director and lead the praise team. I'm back to my first love of singing for the Lord.

Where does that leave *Mary*?

The story of how God chose this ordinary family to serve Him begs to be told. What an adventure God took us on! This book is simply the first step. No, I am not performing *Mary* in its entirety anymore. Gracious, I'd have to be Mary's grandmother, I am that old! It doesn't mean that others couldn't perform it, though. As I write this, making *Mary, the Story of Jesus through His Mother's Eyes* available for performance is in the works.

In the meantime, God has given us an amazing story to tell, the story of an ordinary family serving an extraordinary God. Shalom, Shalom.

Luke 2:7 (CEV) *She gave birth to her firstborn son. She dressed him in baby clothes and laid him on a bed of hay because there was no room for them in the inn.*

Jeremiah 29:11 (CEV) *I will bless you with a future filled with hope—a future of success, not of suffering.*

Lord Lessons

1. Sometimes God has to shut a door or in our case, send a notice that our lease would not be renewed. This caused us to move on in another direction.
2. A closed door can be extremely painful, but waiting on the Lord to open the next one is always worth it. His plans for our life include a future filled with success and hope.
3. Because God sees our life in its entirety, a closed door can be a way of preventing us from making a mistake.
4. Sometimes the only way God can get our attention is by slamming the door shut, locking it, and throwing away the key. This was definitely the case for Jimbo and me with The Stable. God moved drastically.

Questions to Ponder

1. Have you ever had a door of opportunity slam shut? Explain.
2. Looking back, can you now see God's mighty hand at work in your life? How so?
3. What do you do when you find yourself at a cross-roads in your life's journey?

20

Game Boy, Cracker Barrel & Hotel Pools

Chelsea's Story

My parents have been asking my sister and me to write our chapters about *Mary* for years. To be honest, I was young when *Mary* started and I wasn't exactly sure what I would write, or how to write it. And my version of *Mary* is much different as an adolescent than my parents or Kate. But I will start from the top and let the memories flow as I type.

When I think of *Mary*, my first thought is how lucky we were to have had that experience as a family. Not only did we see the entire country (minus North Dakota), but we created memories from the van and RV that we talk about to this day. Whenever anyone asks how my childhood was, or how I was able to see the country my response is "Oh, it was a unique experience!" However, that is the politically correct version. Who doesn't say "Ahh what a great time that was!" when they consider a family vacation or experience? But let's take a deep dive into the memories not everyone talks about, that may be a little unorthodox, and just plain hilarious.

My first memory of *Mary* would be watching my Mom write out the script. I can remember her writing at the kitchen table starting at 5:00 AM and handwriting everything (I have inherited her lack of IT skills, by the way) I was only in 2nd or 3rd grade, and watching her write the script daily was something I couldn't imagine committing to. And when she told me she is "doing *Mary*" as her mother's dying wish, I thought (at 7 years old), "Yikes please don't do this to me someday". The pressure!

The next part I remember is traveling to Nashville to record the album. I mostly remember this because it was my Christmas break from school, and I was slightly annoyed to travel. I wanted to just lay around and play Barbies, and my beloved Sims. Instead of the TV and couches, Kate and I were entertaining ourselves on the floor of a recording studio. Mostly me picking at Kate, I'm sure.

The beginning years of *Mary*, I don't recall much. I was young, and at that point, we were mainly performing at churches in Pennsylvania. I do remember that the performances picked up speed rapidly. It wasn't long before we were traveling every weekend to perform. After a while, Kate and I were allowed to bring a friend along. My elementary school friends still talk about coming with us on the road.

One time I brought Melissa Punk, and there was Esmeralda Chap Stick in the nursery. She thought it was disgusting that I used it. Who would pass up Hunchback of Notre Dame lip stuff? I would also get rather annoyed when I brought a friend and they actually wanted to watch the show. I had brought them along to entertain me! Certainly, I'm not going to be watching *Mary* for the 100th time. But alas, I watched alongside them, and they loved every second of it. The best part of bringing a friend was going out to eat after the performance.

Another time we went to Perkins with Kelly Saquin. She ordered the popcorn shrimp and French fries basket and said something I still use to this day - "you can't go wrong ordering French fries." We also laughed so hard that night with my parents that she fell under the dinner table. Who even knows what it was about?

Speaking of fixations, there was a time during our southern coast tour that I was fixated on...bowling. I have zero reasons as to why I wanted to bowl. I am horrible at it. Like gutter city. Of course, I asked the classic question "Is there a pool at the hotel?" But after 3 years of hotel pools, I wanted to bowl. And bowl badly. So much so that my parents let me join a bowling league in 5th grade (I think to help with my fascination?). I was so obsessed that I actually cried once when we passed an alley, and the neon lights of the lanes dimmed as we kept driving to our destination. Which, sadly, was NOT a bowling alley.

Although being in the back of a van or RV sounds like it would be...challenging with your sibling, Kate and I made the most of it (when I wasn't charging her $1 to play my Game Boy Color). One time we even made a whole musical to the Veggie Tales album and danced up and down the hallway of the RV. We also knew when something "fun and off the itinerary" was coming by the way our Mom would lean into Jimbo and whisper. Typically, that was a stop at Cracker Barrel, but not always! Once she even swam with us at Super 8 (and jumped in!) and convinced him to take us to Hibachi across the street. And don't get us started on the Holiday Inn that has the indoor shuffleboard and Papa Johns.

I could go on and on about our tales in the van and RV. Although those memories are the funniest and most memorable,

I have been known to tell people that my favorite memory of all was watching my Dad watch my Mom perform. Even as a little girl, I knew it was something special to see him beam from ear to ear watching her do her thing on stage. The support was always unconditional, no matter how big and crazy the dream was. There are a million stories to tell and laughs to be had, but the life lessons are priceless and truly unique. I hope you have enjoyed a trip down memory lane from the littlest Lenaway.

{ 21 }

Weird and Wonderful

Kate's Story

I grew up weird. Really weird. Who else can say by age 14 they had travelled to 47 of the 50 states? I've eaten prairie dog, rattlesnake, and alligator. I've seen Wall Drug, and Mount Rushmore and dipped my toes in both oceans. I've stood in four states at once, attempted to look interested at Devil's Tower, and slept through the entire Midwest. That was the good stuff.

The bad? I shared the back seat of a minivan with my younger sister for weeks on end. Never bringing enough reading material. The echoing sounds of my Dad crunching late-night snacks in hotel rooms. Constantly catching up on homework.

I knew I was growing up weird. I knew I was growing up lucky. I knew I was growing up with different goals, dreams, and beliefs than other kids my age. I knew I was growing up with parents who were not just go-getters, they were downright giants of dreaming

{ 102 }

big and achieving. I knew I was seeing our part of the world in such a cool, unique way. I knew firsthand and never doubted the power of prayer and God's plan for our family.

But that doesn't mean that there weren't days I wanted to be home, instant messaging my friends from the family computer in the living room, sitting on a floaty in Katie's pool baking my skin to a nice shade of medium well, eating popcorn late at night while watching "Grease" for the 900th time.

Being a teenager is tough.

Being a teenager in the back seat of a minivan through Nebraska while your Dad plays 90s praise and worship music, your Mom sleeps with her feet on the dash and your sister refuses to let you play her Gameboy color without paying her a dollar is even tougher.

That's really tough. Really weird. But really, really good.

I remember distinctly the last time my Grammie Bonnie spoke to me. She came to our house the night before her second brain surgery. I had just had my first flute lesson of the school year and was so excited to play for her. "Hot Cross Buns", I'm sure. I stood in my parents' kitchen, with my Mom, Dad, and grandparents staring at me, and fumbled my way through the song. Grammie was emotional when I was done. That was the first moment I realized what could happen. What I didn't realize is that it WOULD happen.

My Grammie would pass away a year later.

My life would completely change a year after that.

I've never been the same since my Grammie encouraged... insisted... my Mom write *Mary*. Gram was a force to be reckoned with. She was the wind in the sails that pushed my Mom's ship out to the ocean of the unknown. God was the captain of the ship. My Mom was the diligent first mate, writing, producing, singing, designing, and dreaming. My Dad was in the crow's nest, keeping a watch out for any icebergs and navigating us through the calm and stormy seas. Chelsea and I were swabbing the deck, steerage class passengers along for the journey of our lives.

There's something to be said about growing up weird. I hope I'm raising my own little weirdos to know that what God designs is better than anything we could ever dream. That the world is so much bigger than our little hometown. They come from a family of dreamers, but not just dreamers- doers. That no matter the goal, we will work until it happens. No goal, no dream, no spark of imagination is too crazy when you're growing up weird. Pray about it, believe in it, then get up and do it.

I could ramble on with silly stories about our time on the road, all the places we visited, all the food we've tried, and all the different styles of churches I've experienced. I could tell you about trying lobster in Maine, riding in the ferry to Nantucket and feeling like a character from a WB drama with the wind in my hair and the water spraying in my face (the drama!), playing basketball in the driveway of a random church in Georgia for hours on end while the RV battery charged (I'm really terrible at basketball), my legs having hundreds of mosquito bites from spending a week jammed in a tiny light booth in a New York City black box theatre. I could tell you which denominations had the best cookies, which churches have the nicest Christmas decorations, and how many pastors love to start a welcome speech with "This is the day that the Lord hath made, let us rejoice and be glad in it"(Hint... it's a lot!)

But to me, it's more about growing up weird. I'm grateful to have grown up how I did. I'm blessed to have grown up a believer. A believer in God, the Waymaker, and the Miracle Worker. I know these words to be true because I saw it all with my own eyes. And if that makes me weird, I'll wear that title proudly.

From Addicted to Alcohol to Addicted to Jesus

Jimbo's story.
Mount Union, Pennsylvania

It was 2004, and, for the first time in many years, we weren't involved with the youth group, so I went to the Creation Festival. Beth and the girls couldn't join me, so I took off for a couple of days on my own. I had a fabulous time with the teaching, the small group, - and certainly the music. I volunteered and helped out on a couple of things.

One of my privileged duties was the prayer tent.

Standing in the prayer tent, sweat rolling down my face and back because of the blistering heat, I met some of the Creation staff who coordinate and oversee the prayer portion of the ministry. Boy, I'll tell you, teens, and even some adults who were touched by the teaching, praying, and singing, came to the prayer tent. Their needs were many. They were dealing with some serious issues. I witnessed firsthand just how powerful an event like Creation is to address somber matters.

One memorable young lady, about 17 years old, came in with her friend. She was clearly distraught; her makeup was running-tears streaming down her cheeks. Even her friend was choking back sobs as she was holding on to her because the young lady appeared weak and weighed down by the stress of whatever she was coming to offload. At this time, many, many other teens and adults came into the tent, so I was the only one who was not directly involved in prayer with anyone at that moment. As soon as I saw the young lady heading toward me I realized, whoa! Whatever is causing these tears is serious, and maybe it shouldn't be a male to console her when she is in such an emotional state. It turned out that I had made an accurate assessment. Thankfully, as the young woman came close, I saw one of the staff ladies and got her attention by waving her over. This woman was trained and experienced, so I backed off and just prayed for God's help in the situation. I learned later that, sure enough, the young girl had been abused for years. I didn't get any details but was grateful that she acquired the first step of help and was referred to some qualified folks for follow-up.

After a while, the tent cleared out and slowed down. I began chatting with Julio, one of the other gentlemen who was a volunteer there. I told him about the young woman, and we prayed for her. He also saw some very important decisions being made in lives affected by God that day. We marveled at how God was moving amongst the tens of thousands of people there on that hillside near Mount Union, Pennsylvania. God was healing physical ailments and emotional problems, breaking through to folks who had previously resisted the love and friendship of Jesus. Much of this happened through ordinary people like us serving an extraordinary God.

During our conversation, we talked about how God had moved in our own lives. I said, "Well, for me, it was how I got saved." He asked me to tell him the story.

After I got divorced, I went from a problem drinker to a full-fledged alcoholic. My life was going right down the drain to the point where my bosses held an intervention. They required me to attend Alcoholics Anonymous meetings with a coworker as my sponsor. I tried. Sort of.

I'm in favor of AA now, but I sure wasn't then. I didn't warm up to it at all. One of the things I had a problem with was a "higher power." And how dare they suggest that I was powerless over alcohol- that my life had become unmanageable. Like most addicted people, I was in denial. I sounded a little like, "I can control this. I can quit anytime I want." I didn't want all that religious mumbo jumbo. Well, it turned out that later I realized that I did need all of that.

In the midst of my downward spiral, I met Beth. One day I was talking to her (flirting?) and she told me that she was having a tough time because she and her husband were newly divorced. Bingo! I viewed this as an opportunity, like an open door for me to pursue my interest in her.

Although I liked her a lot, she didn't care for me at all. She was a churchgoer. I hated church. She was a tea totaler. I was a drunk. She sang in the choir. I sang next to the jukebox. You get the picture. I gave her the old line, "Oh no. That's got to be tough. I understand because I've been divorced, and I remember the pain. But it's important to have a friend who can commiserate with you. Call me because I'd love to talk to you and be a good listener during this time." (A little "I'll be your huckleberry pick-up strategy")

Then she says, "Thanks, but I already have someone I talk to." My thought was that she didn't seem like the type of woman who would have a guy as a close confidant- sharing intimate feelings. What's going on here?

So, I asked, "Who is this guy who you are talking to?

And she says, "Jesus."

Just like that. Matter of fact. Right out in the open. It wasn't even Sunday, and we weren't in church.

Well, I say, "What?" Because I was flabbergasted. And she says, "Yes. Jesus is my best friend, and I talk to him anytime I want to."

My jaw dropped. Mind blown. I didn't know how to respond. I'd never heard anyone ever say anything like that even though I'd been to church as a child and a teen a thousand times.

And then she just smiled and walked away!

This idea of friendship with Jesus intrigued me. A lot.

Over the next two months, the thought of having Jesus as your best friend just kept repeating- like a song in my head. Eventually, it began to subside. When November rolled around, I was still out partying with my buddies and failing at the 12 steps. I got plastered most weekends and even on a few weekdays.

On Saturday mornings, I worked part-time as a disc jockey at a radio station. One day a local pastor, John Shimko, heard me on the air being a total idiot- saying inappropriate things. I'd been up all night drinking the night before and rolled into work directly from an all-night booze party. Pastor Shimko was on his way to the radio station to do his on-air 10-minute daily devotion. He brought me a cup of coffee and some doughnuts. We chatted for a while, having a great conversation even though he could clearly see my bleary eyes and I wreaked of booze. To his credit, he didn't beat me over the head with the Bible or tell me how terrible I was acting on the radio. He didn't say anything condemning whatsoever. Instead, he related to me. It turned out we both enjoyed listening to John Denver.

After he finished his on-air devotion, just as he was leaving the station, he said, "Hey you know over at our church we have a worship service tomorrow morning at 11. We'd love to have you join us." So, I said out loud, "Yeah, maybe I'll stop in there." But in my mind, I was thinking, "There's no way I'm going to that church because there's a bunch of Jesus freaks who go there."

Saturday night rolled around, and I went out partying again. On Sunday morning, I met my buddies at 10:00 o'clock at the Hillcrest Restaurant for breakfast. And, as alcoholics often do, we laughed about how drunk and stupid we were the night before. We thought it was a riot.

I finished up my bacon and eggs and headed for the door at around 10 minutes to 11:00. It was one of those glass and aluminum doors typical for a storefront. I had my hand on the doorknob. I looked diagonally across the intersection, and I spotted that church.

Now, this may sound very strange but somehow, all of a sudden, the front door of the restaurant became the front door of the church. I didn't remember or have a conscious awareness of walking over to the church. I was just like there. I don't know how to explain it. Once inside the church, the fog cleared.

"Did I just walk into church?"

My initial reaction was to bolt for the door. I took one step and then was greeted by a friend of mine. My thought was, "Well, I can't leave now." He ushered me down to a pew.

This was all foreign to me. I had no clue what was going on. After a bit, Pastor Shimko went to the pulpit to deliver his message for the morning. He looked over and saw me. I could tell by the look on his face that he was as surprised to see me sitting there as I was to be there!

He set aside whatever it is he had prepared for that Sunday sermon. Then he said to the congregation, "Folks, I'm making a change this morning in our message. Today I want to talk about something else. Please open your Bibles to the Gospel of John, chapter three."

I didn't have any idea where John is in the Bible. This little old lady, about 80 years old, picked up a Bible that was in the pew in front of me. She opened it to John. She handed it to me and pointed to chapter three. I thought, "OK, what am I supposed to do with this?"

The pastor started teaching from John 3:3- Being born again. He worked his way to John 3:16, which I had never heard before. I know that sounds bizarre, especially for someone like me who had spent many a Sunday growing up in church. I guess I never paid any attention to it.

Pastor Shimko gave a phenomenal message about John 3:16 and 17. "For God so loved the world that He gave His only Son, and whoever believes in Him shall not perish but have everlasting life. For God did not send the Son into the world to judge the world, but that the world should be saved through Him."

This was quite backward to me because my understanding of God and Jesus was quite different than what he was sharing. I thought God was mad at me. Obviously, I was wrong. It was amazing to learn that Jesus loved me no matter what.

Wow! This was eye-opening!

At the end of the sermon, Pastor Shimko told everybody to bow their heads and close their eyes. So, we did because you do whatever the pastor says, right? I had my head bowed and my eyes closed while he gave an invitation. I don't remember exactly what he said. He used phrases common within the walls of the church, but uncommon for folks like me outside the church. I didn't really know what he was talking about. He wanted people to respond by raising their hand.

There was this kind of uncomfortable silence. As I sat there, I suspected that he was talking to me because everyone else, of the 60 elderly people in the church, were regulars. A few moments passed and he gave the invitation a second time. Again, another set of "Christianese" phrases I didn't understand. Only, now, I was sure he was talking to me.

I began to ponder that I was pretty interested in John 3:16. Maybe I ought to raise my hand because he assured us that he was not going to embarrass anyone. He just wanted to pray for whoever makes this indication. I thought that this might be OK. But I got this thought that I now believe was planted there by Satan, "Don't you dare raise your hand because if you do, then you're going to have to quit having fun."

Let's be clear, the worldly "fun" I was having was disastrous and self-destructive.

I didn't raise my hand.

Thankfully, Pastor Shimko didn't give up. He knew that he'd hooked one and wanted to reel me in. The fish closest to the boat fights the hardest. That was me. This third time when he gave the invitation, he didn't use the "Christianese" vocabulary.

With confidence, he said, "I know there is someone here today who wants Jesus as their best friend."

Whoa! Instantaneously, my brain went back to Beth telling me about Jesus being her best friend. Nothing Satan said or did could stop me. I shot my hand up because I was hungry to have Jesus as my best friend.

I want to tell you that God was victorious!

So, as I was telling this story to Julio, tears gathered in his eyes (and mine too). He rejoiced about God's victory in my life. Then I asked him, "What about you?" He said, "My story is a little weird. I was given the message of salvation by Mary."

I said, "Who?"

He said, "You know, Mary, the mother of Jesus."

I said, "You've got to tell this story, Julio."

He and his wife were from New York City. They decided to move to South Jersey about 30 miles east of Philadelphia. The first Sunday, they were looking for a church to attend. They saw this nice-looking Come Alive Church and decided to give it a try. During the service, the pastor announced that there was going to be a special program that night. A traveling theater group was coming to put on a musical drama called *Mary, the Story of Jesus through His Mother's Eyes*. You can imagine at this point I was extremely interested in how his story would go.

Julio's wife, Maria, had always held Mary in high regard. So, they decided to return that evening to see the play.

They loved the music, the story, and the way Mary was presented as an ordinary girl who was obedient to God's calling.

Julio said, "Basically, Mary told the whole gospel in one play."

As he told me the story I began to tear up. The more he told me, the more I cried. I'm sure he was thinking that this was a much more powerful story than he ever imagined. Then he says, "At the end of the play, a man got up and encouraged the people in the audience to make the decision to accept Jesus as their best friend. Please talk to a pastor, priest, or minister that you know or come up here to talk to the folks that will pray with you about your decision."

Julio and Maria got up after the play and chatted with one of the pastors of the church. After some prayer, they gave their lives to Christ.

By this time, I was just bawling. Tears were streaming down my face.

"Now," he said, "Whenever anyone asks him, "Who led you to the Lord?", I tell them Jesus' mother Mary."

I could barely breathe, much less speak at that point.

Finally, I told him, "Julio, that was so powerful. Let me tell you why. That was us."

Julio asked, "What do you mean?"

"That Mary was my wife, Beth. And I was the one who came up after the performance to give the invitation."

Well, between cheering and crying and hugging and high-fiving each other the people around us probably thought that the Holy Spirit sure got ahold of these two dudes or we were going crazy.

I was so appreciative that God allowed that "chance" meeting to happen. With 100,000 people at Creation Fest, I just "happened" to bump into a guy we ministered to several years before. Beth and I needed to know about Julio because during the 10 years out on the road in ministry we would show up at a church, a school, an auditorium, or a park to plant the seeds. We delivered the message of love. Then a few hours later, we would pack up and hustle off to the next place. We rarely received feedback to let us know we were doing good for God's Kingdom.

Julio confirmed that day that if we are obedient to what God wants us to do, if we get the good news out there, and even if it's not perfect, then the Holy Spirit will take that seed and bring it to life. It will multiply.

As you are finishing reading *On the Road with Mary*, I want to take this moment to assure you of two things:

First, if you haven't yet, please make the decision to fall in love with Jesus.

Second, whatever it is that God wants you to do- your God job- please just do it. (John 2:5)

It will have an effect on the Kingdom. There is something special that God wants you to do. (Ephesians 2:10) So, right now tell God that you'll do it. Make the decision to do whatever it is he wants you to do. Here I am Lord, send me. (Isaiah 6:8)

And always remember- Jesus loves you, NO MATTER WHAT.

Thanks

Beth as Mary singing a lullaby to baby Jesus.

Thanks for joining us on our journey
"On the Road with Mary."

Visit us at OrdinaryPeopleMin.org
for information on other books and live appearances.

Milton Keynes UK
Ingram Content Group UK Ltd.
UKHW040708201123
432908UK00001B/196